Paul Hattaway, a native _ New Zealand, has served the Church in Asia for most of his life. He is an expert on the Chinese Church, and author of *The Heavenly Man*, *An Asian Harvest*, *Operation China*, *Shandong*, *Guizhou* and many other books. He and his wife Joy are the founders of Asia Harvest (<www.asiaharvest.org>), which supports thousands of indigenous missionaries and has provided millions of Bibles to Christians throughout Asia.

# Also by Paul Hattaway:

*The Heavenly Man*

*An Asian Harvest*

*Operation China*

*China's Christian Martyrs*

*Shandong*

*Guizhou*

# ZHEJIANG

*The Jerusalem of China*

Paul Hattaway

First published in Great Britain in 2019
Also published in 2019 by Asia Harvest, www.asiaharvest.org

Society for Promoting Christian Knowledge
36 Causton Street
London SW1P 4ST
www.spck.org.uk

The author and publisher have made every effort to ensure that the external website
and email addresses included in this book are correct and up to date at the time of
going to press. The author and publisher are not responsible for the content, quality
or continuing accessibility of the sites.

Author's agent: The Piquant Agency, 183 Platt Lane, Manchester M14 7FB, UK

*British Library Cataloguing-in-Publication Data*
A catalogue record for this book is available from the British Library

ISBN 978–0–281–08034–2
eBook ISBN 978–0–281–08035–9

1 3 5 7 9 10 8 6 4 2

Typeset by Fakenham Prepress Solutions, Fakenham, Norfolk NR21 8NL


eBook by Fakenham Prepress Solutions, Fakenham, Norfolk NR21 8NL

# *Zhejiang*

---

## 浙江

### "Silent River"

*Map of China showing Zhejiang Province*

## Zhejiang

| | |
|---|---|
| **Pronounced:** | Zheh-jahng |
| **Old spelling:** | Chekiang |
| **Population:** | 45,930,651 (2000) |
| | 54,426,891 (2010) |
| | 62,923,131 (2020) |
| **Area:** | 39,300 sq. miles (101,800 sq. km) |
| **Population density:** | 1,601 people per sq. mile (618 per sq. km) |
| **Highest elevation:** | 6,329 feet (1,929 meters) |
| **Capital city:** | Hangzhou 5,162,093 |

**Other cities (2010):**

| | |
|---|---|
| Wenzhou | 2,686,825 |
| Ningbo | 2,583,073 |
| Taizhou | 1,189,276 |
| Cixi | 1,059,942 |
| Rui'an | 927,383 |
| Yiwu | 878,903 |
| Jiaxing | 762,643 |

**Administrative divisions:**

| | |
|---|---|
| Prefectures: | 11 |
| Counties: | 90 |
| Towns: | 1,570 |

**Major ethnic groups (2000):**

| | | *Percent* |
|---|---|---|
| Han Chinese | 45,535,266 | 98.8 |
| She | 170,993 | 0.5 |
| Tujia | 55,310 | 0.2 |
| Miao | 53,418 | 0.2 |
| Bouyei | 21,457 | 0.1 |
| Hui | 19,609 | 0.1 |

# Contents

# Contents

# Foreword

Over many years and generations, the followers of Jesus in China have set their hearts to be the witnesses of Christ to the nation. Many have paid a great price for their ministry, and the brutal persecutions they have endured for the faith have often been unimaginable.

The Bible commands all believers to "Go into all the world and preach the gospel to all creation" (Mark 16.15). Many foreign missionaries responded to this command in the past, traveling to China to proclaim the Word of God. They blessed the land with their message of new life in Christ, and also suffered greatly when the darkness clashed with God's light. Their faithful service in spite of great hardship was a beautiful example for Chinese believers to emulate as they served God.

China today still urgently needs more servants and laborers to take the gospel throughout the land. God is looking for people who will stand up and declare, "Lord, here am I. Please send me!"

The day of our Lord is near. May your hearts be encouraged by the testimonies of what the Lord Jesus Christ has done in China, to the praise of His glorious Name!

May the Lord raise up more testimonies that would glorify His Name in our generation, the next generation, and for evermore!

Lord, You are the victorious King. Blessed are those who follow You to the end!

*A humble servant of Christ,*
*Moses Xie (1918–2011)\**

* The late Moses Xie wrote this Foreword for the China Chronicles prior to his death in 2011. He was a highly respected Chinese house church leader who spent 23 years of his life in prison for the Name of Jesus Christ.

# The China Chronicles overview

Many people are aware of the extraordinary explosion of Christianity throughout China in recent decades, with the Church now numbering in excess of 100 million members. Few, however, know how this miracle has occurred. The China Chronicles series is an ambitious project to document the advance of Christianity in each province of China from the time the gospel was first introduced to the present day.

The genesis for this project came at a meeting I attended in the year 2000, where leaders of the Chinese house church movements expressed the need for their members to understand how God established His kingdom throughout China.

As a result, it is planned that these books will be translated into Chinese and distributed widely among the Church, both in China and overseas. Millions of Chinese Christians know little of their spiritual legacy, and my prayer is that multitudes would be strengthened, edified and challenged to carry the torch of the Holy Spirit to their generation.

My intention is not to present readers with a dry list of names and dates but to bring alive the marvelous stories of how God has caused His kingdom to take root and flourish in the world's most populated country.

I consider it a great honor to write these books, especially as I have been entrusted, through hundreds of hours of interviews conducted throughout China, with many testimonies that have never previously been shared in public.

Another reason for compiling the China Chronicles is simply to have a record of God's mighty acts in China.

As a new believer in the 1980s, I recall reading many reports from the Soviet Union of how Christian men and women were being brutally persecuted, yet the kingdom of God grew, with many people meeting Jesus Christ. By the time the Soviet empire collapsed in the early 1990s, no one had systematically recorded the glorious deeds of the Holy Spirit during the Communist era. Tragically, the body of Christ has largely forgotten the miracles God performed in those decades behind the Iron Curtain, and we are much the poorer for it.

Consequently, I am determined to preserve a record of God's mighty acts in China, so that future generations of believers can learn about the wonderful events that have transformed tens of millions of lives there.

At the back of each volume will appear a detailed statistical analysis estimating the number of Christians living in every city and county within each province of China. This is the first comprehensive survey into the number of believers in China—in every one of its more than 2,400 cities and counties—in nearly a century.

Such a huge undertaking would be impossible without the cooperation and assistance of numerous organizations and individuals. I apologize to the many people who helped me in various ways whose names are not mentioned here, many because of security concerns. May the Lord be with you and bless you!

I appreciate the help of mission organizations such as the International Mission Board, Overseas Missionary Fellowship (OMF), Revival Chinese Ministries International (RCMI), The Voice of the Martyrs (VOM) and many others that graciously allowed me access to their archives, libraries, photographs, collections and personal records. I am indebted to the many believers whose generosity exemplifies Jesus' command, "Freely you have received; freely give" (Matthew 10.8).

Many Chinese believers, too numerous to list, have lovingly assisted in this endeavor. For example, I fondly recall the aged house church evangelist Elder Fu, who required two young men to assist him up the stairs to my hotel room because he was eager to be interviewed for this series. Although he had spent many years in prison for the gospel, this saint desperately wanted to testify to God's great works so that believers around the world could be inspired and encouraged to live a more consecrated life. Countless Chinese believers I met and interviewed were similarly keen to share what God has done, to glorify His Name.

Finally, it would be remiss not to thank the Lord Jesus Christ. As you read these books, my prayer is that He will emerge from the pages not merely as a historical figure, but as Someone ever present, longing to seek and to save the lost by displaying His power and transformative grace.

Today the Church in China is one of the strongest in the world, both spiritually and numerically. Yet little more than a century ago China was considered one of the most difficult mission fields. The great Welsh missionary Griffith John once wrote:

> The good news is moving but very slowly. The people are as hard as steel. They are eaten up both soul and body by the world, and do not seem to feel that there can be reality in anything beyond sense. To them our doctrine is foolishness, our talk jargon. We discuss and beat them in argument. We reason them into silence and shame; but the whole effort falls upon them like showers upon a sandy desert.[1]

How things have changed! When it is all said and done, no person in China will be able to take credit for the amazing revival that has occurred. It will be clear that this great accomplishment is the handiwork of none other than the Lord Jesus Christ. We will stand in awe and declare:

The LORD has done this,
  and it is marvelous in our eyes.
This is the day the LORD has made;
  let us rejoice and be glad in it.
     (Psalm 118.23–24, NIV 1984)

*Paul Hattaway*

*Publisher's note*: In the China Chronicles we have avoided specific information, such as individuals' names or details that could lead directly to the identification of house church workers. The exceptions to this rule are where a leader has already become so well known around the world that there is little point concealing his or her identity in these books. This same principle applies to the use of photographs.

Several different systems for writing the sounds of Chinese characters in English have been used over the years, the main ones being the Wade-Giles system (introduced in 1912) and Pinyin (literally "spelling sounds"), which has been the accepted form in China since 1979. In the China Chronicles, all names of people and places are given in their Pinyin form, although in many instances the old spelling is also given in parentheses. This means that the places formerly spelt Chung-king, Shantung and Tien-tsin are now respectively Chongqing, Shandong and Tianjin; Mao Tse-tung becomes Mao Zedong, and so on. The only times we have retained the old spelling of names is when they are part of the title of a published book or article listed in the Notes or Bibliography.

# Introduction

## *A small, influential province*

Zhejiang, which means "Silent River," derives its name from the Qiantang River which flows past the capital city of Hangzhou before emptying into Hangzhou Bay.

Although in size Zhejiang is one of the smallest provinces in China, it had the tenth highest population at the time of the 2010 census, with 54.4 million people. Due to rapid immigration from other parts of China, Zhejiang's population is expected to exceed approximately 62 million by 2020.

With an area of just over 39,000 square miles (101,800 sq. km), Zhejiang is slightly smaller than the US state of Kentucky, but contains approximately 13 times as many people. By another comparison, Zhejiang covers an area about 80 percent the size of England, and contains a slightly higher population.

For centuries Zhejiang has been culturally divided into two broad categories of people. The inland mountainous parts of the province remained impoverished for many generations, while millions of families earned a good living from fishing and trading along the coastline of the East China Sea, which has more than 18,000 offshore islands (the most of any province in China). The coastal people were shaped by contact with the outside world and its ideas, customs and religions.

For many centuries the capital city, Hangzhou, has been regarded as a place of great natural beauty, which gave rise to a famous Chinese saying: "Heaven above, Suzhou and Hangzhou beneath." Indeed, the whole province of Zhejiang has been described as a place of "great beauty and variety: forest-clad

1

mountains and hills, lovely rivers and streams, ancient bridges of architectural charm, bamboo groves, vineyards, world-famous tea plantations and walled cities of which Hangzhou, the capital, is the queen."[1]

Although the history of Hangzhou City dates back to the start of the Qin Dynasty (221 BC), many centuries passed before Zhejiang came to national attention. The rulers of the Tang Dynasty (AD 618–907) were "the first to pay much attention to the Zhejiang and Fujian coastal regions, and they brought them fully into the Sinitic world."[2] The region was first connected to the rest of China when the Grand Canal reached its southern terminus in the province in the seventh century.

After Zhejiang gained a reputation for its bountiful harvests, millions of tons of produce were transported along the canal to other parts of China, feeding the impoverished northern masses during times of famine. The people of Zhejiang benefited financially from the natural bounty of their land, and many areas became wealthy. The province also gained the nickname "the Land of Silk" during this time, and today Zhejiang still produces more than a third of China's raw silk.

## *A patchwork of languages*

Prior to the seventh century, Zhejiang was inhabited by a myriad of different ethno-linguistic groups. Some were the ancestors of minority groups still found in China today, while others exhibited a curious mixture of tribal and Chinese culture. Dialects and languages changed frequently as travelers made their way through the province, so that even villagers living on opposite banks of a river spoke different dialects and struggled to communicate with one another.

When early Evangelical missionaries arrived in Zhejiang they too struggled with the linguistic barriers. The southern parts of the province were home to a complex collection of languages and dialects, including the Min varieties spoken by millions of people across the border in Fujian. In 1878 the mission magazine *China's Millions* noted:

> In the south of Zhejiang, as in the west, the spoken dialects are so peculiar that to work effectually, the dialects of most of the districts have to be specially acquired by both native and foreign laborers. On this account our progress is rendered comparatively slow, and our stations as yet are but few.[3]

Even within the same regions of Zhejiang, linguistic varieties were markedly different. The Wenzhou dialect, for example, is so different from other Zhejiang varieties that during China's war with Vietnam in 1979, the Chinese military employed Wenzhou soldiers to communicate secure information, in much the same way as the United States engaged Navajo "code-talkers" to confuse the Japanese during the Second World War.

After the collapse of the Tang Dynasty in AD 907, a new period known as the Five Dynasties and Ten Kingdoms emerged. Although these kingdoms lasted only 53 years, boundaries were established along linguistic lines that can still be seen today. Historian Leo Moser noted: "Along the coast, the territory of the kingdom of Wu-Yue included almost exactly those parts of Zhejiang and Jiangsu provinces where the Wu sub-language is now spoken."[4]

Wu was established as the dominant spoken Chinese language in Zhejiang. Only in recent decades has Mandarin emerged to threaten its dominance, having become the national standard for all education and media after the founding of the People's Republic of China.

Wu continues to be spoken by approximately 90 million people in China today, more than half of whom live in Zhejiang. It was considered so different from other Chinese varieties that missionaries deemed it necessary to produce a distinct translation of the Bible in the Wu language in the early twentieth century.

Other Chinese languages spoken in Zhejiang include Min Nan (also known as Hokkien), which spills across the southern border from Fujian Province; Hakka; and Huizhou, which is spoken only in Chun'an County near Hangzhou.

## *The golden era*

The greatest era in the history of Zhejiang occurred during the Southern Song Dynasty (1127–1279). To this day, the province is renowned throughout China because of the glory afforded to it during its golden period almost nine centuries ago.

Due to the invasion of northern "barbarian" tribes, the new rulers of China, based in Beijing, sought to govern from a safer location, so thousands of bureaucrats and scholars traveled

*The Grand Canal at the ancient town of Xitang in northern Zhejiang*

down the Grand Canal to Hangzhou, making it their new capital city. The population of Hangzhou is believed to have grown from 500,000 to nearly two million people in just a few decades.

By the time Marco Polo visited Hangzhou (which he called Kinsay) in the early 1280s, the Italian was overwhelmed by its grandeur, calling it "beyond dispute the finest and noblest city in the world."[5] When his descriptions reached Europe, most people refused to believe that a city in the Orient could be far more advanced than Venice, which they considered beyond compare. Many accused Polo of exaggeration, but subsequent findings and the testimony of other early visitors have supported his claims. Polo described Hangzhou and its people in detail, saying:

> The city is so great that it has a hundred miles of compass. And there are in it 12,000 bridges of stone, for the most part so lofty that a great fleet could pass beneath them. And let no man marvel that there are so many bridges, for you see the whole city stands as if it were in the water and surrounded by water, so that a great many bridges are required to give free passage about it . . .
>
> Inside the city there is a lake which has a compass of some 30 miles: and all around it are erected beautiful palaces and mansions, of the richest and most exquisite structure that you can imagine, belonging to the nobles of the city. There are also on its shores many abbeys and churches [temples] of the Idolaters. In the middle of the lake are two islands, on each of which stands a rich, beautiful and spacious edifice, furnished in such a style as to seem fit for the palace of an emperor.[6]

## The Taiping destruction

Millions of people have moved into Zhejiang from other parts of China over the centuries, but some of the more significant migrations occurred in the seventeenth century, when the Min Nan seafaring peoples from Fujian Province colonized the Zhejiang coast. Not only did they bring their distinctive language, but also a myriad of unique customs and a host of female deities.

During the eighteenth century the city of Wenzhou grew to national prominence and gained a reputation as a center of great wealth. Dominating the trade routes of the day, merchant ships sailed from Wenzhou to much of the known world, trading with Japan, Indonesia, India and even along the east coast of Africa.

The people of Zhejiang continued to prosper until the Taiping Rebellion from 1850 to 1864, which brought massive devastation to the province. In many towns and counties in western Zhejiang, "90 percent of the inhabitants were killed and villages were totally depopulated."[7] Large tracts of fertile land were left abandoned, which attracted a new wave of migrants from other provinces. Millions entered from Fujian in the south, while others came from the north and west. The Taiping rebels laid siege to the beautiful capital, Hangzhou, "reduced almost the entire city to ashes, annihilated or displaced most of the population, and finally ended Hangzhou's significance as a commercial and trading center."[8]

## Zhejiang today

Like most of China, Zhejiang suffered greatly during the excesses of the Cultural Revolution (1966–76), but the province rebounded strongly and is today looked upon with admiration and envy by many people in poorer parts of China. The province's economic output has become so great in recent decades that people often speak of the "Zhejiang spirit" when describing the work ethic needed to succeed in business.

Zhejiang's major cities are the economic powerhouses of the province. The capital city Hangzhou is home to more than five million people, while Wenzhou, Ningbo and Shaoxing also contribute to the great wealth of the region. Despite ranking 26th in size and tenth in population among China's provinces, Zhejiang boasts the fourth highest gross domestic product (GDP), with only Guangdong, Jiangsu and Shandong providing a greater boost to the national economy. Indeed, Zhejiang's importance to China's prosperity can be seen in the fact that its GDP nearly matches that of the combined output of the massive Beijing and Shanghai municipalities.

During the 1960s and 1970s, the Chinese government believed that if the military in the renegade province of Taiwan should attack the mainland, the most likely target for invasion would be the coastal areas of Zhejiang, especially the city of Wenzhou. As a result:

> The people of Wenzhou grew accustomed to fending for themselves, beginning first by learning how to produce small consumer items like shoes and umbrellas, which they sold on the side to help them subsidize their meagre incomes. These items were made in small home or village operations . . . and eager Wenzhou natives traveled to different parts of the country to sell their wares . . .
>
> In 1984, when Deng Xiaoping opened the door for the city to become a coastal development area, the Wenzhou people were quick to establish their own manufacturing and commercial centers. Today the city produces electrical appliances and machinery; plastic, metal, chemical and leather products; and clothing and textiles.
>
> Wenzhou businessmen have a reputation for being enterprising, to say the least, and are well known for their aggressive and cut-throat approach to business. They have also established a wide range of business interests overseas, including restaurants, retail shops and wholesale distributorships.[9]

In recent decades, multitudes of migrant workers from across China have surged into Zhejiang in search of work. As a result, the population of Wenzhou Prefecture grew markedly from 7.5 million to 9.1 million in the decade between 2000 and 2010. Province-wide, the population mushroomed by more than eight million people over the same period. The massive influx of mostly impoverished farmers has created social challenges for Zhejiang, as many migrants found it more difficult to achieve their dreams than they imagined. Multitudes have ended up homeless, and crime has escalated.

Zhejiang is one of China's most ethnically cohesive provinces. Remarkably, 98.8 percent of its people are Han Chinese. The only ethnic minority groups with significant populations in the province are the She people (170,000 people or 0.5 percent) and the Tujia and Miao, who each number approximately 50,000 people. All three of these groups have become highly Sinicized and are not easily distinguishable from the Han in the locations where they live. Even Hui Muslims, who are found scattered throughout every province of China, scarcely make a mark in Zhejiang with a population of only 20,000 people.

# Early Christians in Zhejiang

*A Chinese depiction of Odoric of Pordenone, who discovered many Christians in Zhejiang in the 1320s*

The Nestorians, also known as the Church of the East, are generally held to be the first Christians in China. The Nestorian Stone, which was unearthed near the city of Xi'an in Shaanxi Province, describes how the first Nestorian missionary, Alopen, traveled down the Silk Road from Persia (now Iran) or Syria and introduced the gospel to China in AD 635.

The Nestorians initially found favor with the emperor, who permitted them to teach their doctrine and build churches. They gradually expanded throughout the empire, and Nestorian communities sprang up in a number of trading centers, including several commercial hubs along the east China coast. One of the largest Christian communities was located at Zaitun (now Quanzhou) in Fujian Province, approximately 380 miles (620 km) south of Hangzhou.

The main port for the great city of Hangzhou at the time was located at nearby Ganpu, where the Qiantang River empties into the ocean. Ships regularly sailed from Ganpu to destinations throughout Asia and the world. Merchants and migrants arrived in China via the same port, and thriving communities of Arabs, Jews and Nestorian Christians emerged.

An Arab visitor to Zhejiang during the Tang Dynasty told of a massacre at Ganpu in AD 878, led by a group of rebels who were part of a secret society. The traveler detailed the mass slaughter of the population of Ganpu, and in the process provided the first documented evidence of Christians in Zhejiang:

> The people of Ganpu, having closed their gates, the rebels besieged them for a long while. The town was at length taken, and the inhabitants put to the sword . . . On this occasion there perished 120,000 persons—Muslims, Jews, Christians, and Magi [probably Persians], who had settled in the city for the sake of trade; not to mention the numbers killed who were natives of the country. The number of persons of the four religions mentioned who perished is known, because the Chinese government levied a tax upon them according to their number . . .
>
> There were at Ganpu a great number of Christians; and they were massacred along with the multitude of foreigners who flocked thither to traffic on the coast of China, and usually to the port of Ganpu.[1]

For the next 400 years all mention of Christians in Zhejiang subsided, and it was not until Marco Polo visited Hangzhou in the early 1280s that evidence emerged of the survival of the Christian faith, with Polo briefly mentioning: "There is one church only, belonging to the Nestorian Christians."[2]

Another four decades elapsed before the Italian Franciscan friar, Odoric of Pordenone (1286–1331), passed through Hangzhou and other parts of Zhejiang. He wrote: "In the land there are many Christians, but more Saracens [Muslims] and idolaters."[3]

Alas, the influence of the Nestorians waned soon after this time. The movement is believed to have become bogged down in sin and compromise, before persecution decimated its churches. The Roman Catholics soon found themselves to be the only adherents of any Christian creed still active in China. Their presence in Zhejiang was minimal, however, and by 1663—more than three centuries after Odoric's visit—only 1,000 Catholics reportedly lived in the entire province, a number which increased to 3,000 by 1703.[4]

Later, early Evangelical missionaries in Zhejiang told a number of interesting stories that suggested a remnant of Nestorianism had survived in the province. In 1852 a missionary in Ningbo, J. Goddard, reported:

> A respectable-looking stranger came into our chapel, and listened with much apparent attention to the sermon. After service he stopped to converse. He said that he and his ancestors had worshipped only one God. He knew of Moses, and Jesus, and Mary; said he was neither a Catholic nor Muslim; neither had he seen our books, but that the doctrine was handed down from his ancestors. He did not know where they had obtained it, nor for how many generations they had followed it.[5]

# 1840s

## The first Evangelicals face a toxic atmosphere

Catholic missionaries established work in Zhejiang in the 1600s, and Nestorian Christians were known to have flourished along the coast many centuries before that, but the first Evangelical missionary only set foot in Zhejiang in 1843, when D. J. MacGowan of the American Baptist Missionary Union arrived in the large city of Ningbo.

The American Presbyterians commenced work in Zhejiang a year later in June 1844, when Divie McCartee also settled in Ningbo. At about the same time a single English lady, Mary

*Divie McCartee, one of the first Evangelical missionaries in Zhejiang*

Ann Aldersey, became the first female Evangelical missionary to live in China. She opened a school for girls in Ningbo, which is believed to be the first girls' school in the history of China.

Ningbo was the default location for missionaries at the time, as the British and American governments had already established consulates in the city as a result of military pressure exerted during the Opium Wars. Ningbo was one of five cities along the east China coast declared "treaty ports," which gave British citizens the right to reside in those cities.

The concessions granted to the British by the war settlement caused much festering anger among the Chinese population, and even though the treaty now permitted missionaries the right to reside in Ningbo, they soon encountered a strong resistance to their presence. The years before the missionaries' arrival had witnessed several tense incidents in the province. When a British ship, the *Kite*, ran aground off the coast of Zhejiang in 1841, an English lady, Mrs. Noble, "was carried about the streets in a cage and exhibited to the populace. And at Yuyao . . . the Chinese general flayed and burned alive a foreigner caught during the year of 1841."[1]

Divie McCartee, meanwhile, found that living in the center of Ningbo came with too many distractions. He managed to rent some rooms in a Daoist monastery near the city, and the peaceful environment helped him make good progress in acquiring the language. McCartee's relationship with the Daoist monks was described as "pleasant":

> They were happy to receive the $6 a month rent for the two rooms which McCartee used as a residence and dispensary. The stream of patients probably enhanced the reputation of the monastery. They took no offense at the Christian tracts McCartee displayed, and from the younger monks McCartee learned a good deal of the Ningbo dialect, customs and legends.[2]

13

In one four-month period, the missionary-doctor treated 5,000 patients and performed 90 operations. McCartee enthusiastically reported that he had been "proclaiming from house to house the glad tidings that there is a 'balm in Gilead,' and a physician there who can heal the worst maladies and minister comfort and healing to the wounded spirit."[3]

China at the time was a myriad of different cultures and languages. There was no standard national language, and in Zhejiang Province alone several distinct varieties of Chinese were spoken. As a result, the early missionaries found it necessary to learn the main languages of the town they resided in. One of the early pioneers in Ningbo, William Martin, employed two local language teachers whom he rotated, enabling him to learn the Ningbo dialect both day and night. A historian noted:

> Since the Ningbo dialect could not be accurately represented by Mandarin-based Chinese characters, Martin devised a phonetic system, using Roman letters, to write it out, and soon had formed a society to produce it, as an aid for missionaries in acquiring the language. They also taught the Chinese to use the phonetic system . . . The Chinese "saw with astonishment their children taught to read in a few days, instead of spending years in painful toil, as they must with the native characters. Old women of three-score and ten, and illiterate servants and laborers, on their conversion, found by this means their eyes opened to read in their own tongue."[4]

## *Bao Youyi—the first Chinese preacher in Zhejiang*

Although many Chinese were hostile to the missionaries and their message, some were searching for truth, and a few individuals repented of their sins and placed their trust in Jesus Christ. The first Evangelical fellowship was organized on Zhejiang soil in May 1845.

*A sketch of Bao Youyi preaching on the streets of Ningbo*

Irishman William Russell—who was later appointed the Anglican Bishop of North China—was one of the first Evangelical missionaries in Zhejiang. After the first two Chinese converts were baptized in Ningbo, Russell wrote:

> I cannot help but feeling that the Lord is having His way prepared among this people, and that ere long, if spared, we shall be privileged to see His truth telling largely upon them . . . For the last few weeks I have been in the habit of going out once or twice a week into the neighboring villages and towns, distributing tracts and preaching. Had I physical power, each day I might have addressed some 20 different assemblies, varying in number from 50 to 200 persons, who in most cases would have listened attentively to me for half an hour.[5]

Russell was accompanied on his preaching journeys to the countryside by the first Chinese convert in Ningbo, a man named Bao Youyi. Bao proved to be a vital co-worker to Russell, and was especially effective at presenting the gospel to followers of Confucius, who argued that Jesus is a foreign god and therefore not relevant to the people of China. Bao skillfully yet respectfully stated the truth of Christ, and many listeners were impressed enough to give a hearing to the new teaching. On numerous occasions Russell and Bao had detailed and vigorous exchanges with the people of Zhejiang, like this account of William Russell pleading with locals to believe:

> "My friends, you are already falling into the dark and terrific pit of destruction, and neither Confucius, Mencius, or other sages can save you. Only the power and wisdom of God can save you. Christ Jesus is that power; Christ Jesus is that wisdom . . . Remember that Christianity is not a foreign creed. We foreigners are but letter-carriers and heralds. The letter, the message, comes from heaven. See the setting sun. Is it a native sun or a foreign sun?"
>
> The crowd laughs. "We suppose you foreigners, too, are warmed by it."
>
> "Certainly so. There are native and foreign candles, but only one sun. And when day dawns and the sun is up, blow out your candles. And so when the doctrine of Jesus comes, then all human creeds are needed no longer. O my friends . . . believe in the light! Come, believe in Jesus."[6]

Bao was a tailor by trade, and when he heard the gospel being preached in his town he embraced it. His progress greatly encouraged Russell, who employed him as a catechist to accompany him on his preaching tours. The missionary wrote that Bao had:

> given much satisfaction by his industry and good behavior. His views of the great truths of Christianity seem clearer, and

his acquaintance with Scripture larger than the other converts. But this may arise only from his natural superiority of intellect, he being a very clear-headed and sharp-sighted fellow. He is, I trust, equally sincere in his acknowledgement of Jesus alone, as his only and all-sufficient Savior.[7]

Alas, the trust that William Russell and the other missionaries had placed in Bao appears to have been too hasty, and they were pained to discover that the illiterate man had many character flaws that emerged under the pressure of gospel ministry. He was quick to lose his temper with people, and sometimes his language degenerated to include unwholesome words. The missionaries had expected too much from their first convert, and they saw that, as with all Christians, time was needed for the Holy Spirit to shape and form Bao's character.

Although the two men remained closely connected, Russell placed Bao on probation for three months after one outburst. Although Bao received the decision with a humble attitude, the probation extended to 16 years. Russell and the other early missionaries had hoped Bao might become the first ordained church leader in the province, but their hopes were delayed indefinitely, and their unrealistic expectations were never fulfilled.

Bao Youyi lived until 1874, when he again expressed his trust in Jesus Christ on his deathbed. He was laid to rest in a quiet spot, with his friend and mentor William Russell grieving for the loss of his first Chinese convert.

## Walter Lowrie

The honor of being the first Evangelical martyr in China belongs to the American Walter Lowrie, who was the son of a famous politician from Butler, Pennsylvania. Lowrie's father, Walter Lowrie, Sr., represented Pennsylvania in the US Senate

*Walter Lowrie*

from 1819 to 1825. On the expiration of his term he was elected Secretary of the Senate, an office he held for 12 years. He engaged in politics with the fear of God, and founded the Congressional prayer meetings. His eldest son John was a missionary to India, while Walter Jr. volunteered to serve in China after graduating from Princeton Theological Seminary in November 1841.

Walter Lowrie sailed for China in January 1842, aged just 22. He arrived at Macau and remained in the Portuguese colony for two years, spending his time studying the Chinese language while also indulging his passion for the Scriptures. Lowrie could read both Hebrew and Greek, and was highly respected by his fellow missionaries for his knowledge and humble demeanor.

In April 1844 Lowrie sailed up the coast to Zhejiang Province and took up residence in the Ningbo monastery with Divie McCartee. The Ningbo Mission was duly formed that year with a total of eight missionaries, and a printing press was brought in by ship. In its first two years of operation, 635,000 pages were published and distributed—mostly gospel tracts and Scripture portions. Not long after his arrival in Zhejiang, Lowrie wrote:

> The people are as civil and obliging as could reasonably be expected, considering the severe and uncalled for treatment they received during the war, and the thoughtless course of some English officers, in destroying the public buildings for firewood. We are better treated here, by far, than a Chinaman would be in New York or London; though it does occasionally ruffle one's temper to hear himself called a ... "white devil," with some other such choice epithets.[8]

In 1847 Lowrie was invited to attend a meeting in Shanghai. During the conference a messenger arrived from Ningbo asking him to return immediately because of an emergency. Lowrie left Shanghai on August 16, crossing Hangzhou Bay in a small vessel. His servant recalled what happened next:

> Suddenly, a pirate ship was seen bearing down upon their small craft. Discharging their firearms, the pirates boarded the ship with swords and spears plundering everything in sight. Concerned that the foreigner would testify against them they decided to throw him overboard. He was pushed over the rail ... Lowrie floated around in the water for some time and then sank out of sight.[9]

Walter Lowrie was dead at the age of just 28. When the people in his home church in Pennsylvania heard the tragic news they were shocked and grief-stricken. In 1850 Lowrie's father published a huge 504-page book entitled *Memoirs of the Rev. Walter M. Lowrie, Missionary to China*.[10] Tens of thousands of copies were printed and many Christians committed their lives more fully to God, while unbelievers saw in Lowrie's testimony what a true Christian life was like, and they believed for the first time.

# 1850s

## Recruits from afar

As the 1850s unfolded, Evangelical missionaries began to trickle into Zhejiang. One of the new recruits was William Aitchison, who was born in Glasgow, Scotland, but raised in Connecticut after his family emigrated to the United States.

After gaining work in a factory, Aitchison heard the gospel and surrendered his life to Christ. In due course the Holy Spirit called the young man to serve in China, and after arriving in 1854, he made his way to Pinghu in northeast Zhejiang.

*William Aitchison*

Aitchison became proficient in Chinese and began sharing the gospel with the people of Pinghu. His excitement at finally being able to communicate God's Word was tempered with the realization that it would take time to break up the hard ground of a people with no inclination to seek the Savior of the world. Aitchison reported:

> For upwards of three weeks we have gone almost daily into the city and delivered our message in the most crowded thorough-fares. Our audiences listen with much apparent interest, and the intellectual knowledge of Christianity is plainly on the increase. The numbers who come for private conversation is also much larger than at the outset. In a few cases we have almost hoped that the Holy Spirit was commencing His awakening work on the heart, but as yet we can speak confidently of none.[1]

Months went by, with Aitchison growing increasingly frustrated at the lack of progress. In 1856 he wrote home:

> The gross darkness in which the heathen mind is enveloped is strikingly exhibited in the inquiries proposed or remarks made . . . Preach to them Christ and Him crucified, relate the story of His birth, His instructions, His miracles, His death; show the need of an atonement of sin, and the way in which the Son of God provided it; and when you have finished the discourse, someone will inquire if Christ is the King of England. Talk of the soul, its nature and destiny, the bliss or woe that await it, the wisdom of lightly esteeming this world and of seeking heaven's happiness, and not unlikely some apparently serious person will interrupt you by begging to know the price of your coat.[2]

Aitchison didn't give up, however, and with typical Scottish tenacity he continued to share the good news with as many people as possible. His frustrations gradually gave way, and he gained a firm belief that he was experiencing the very first drops of rain in what would one day become a mighty flood of God's blessing in Zhejiang. He wrote:

> Acquaintances are beginning to be formed. Prejudice is wearing away. The report of our doctrines and object is spreading in all directions. We see the first faint glimmer of that light which is destined to increase more and more unto the perfect day . . . We are not without the hope that our residence here, unimportant as it may seem to some, will be followed by a blessing whose consequences will extend beyond the immediate circle of our operations.[3]

A century and a half later, his predictions have been fulfilled in a marvelous way, and today Zhejiang boasts the highest percentage of Christians of any province in China. Although William Aitchison was forced to leave Pinghu in 1858 when political forces necessitated his evacuation, he had faithfully tilled the soil and scattered the seed of God's Word in a province that had experienced almost no gospel light up to that time.

## *Early Chinese disciples*

Many of the earliest Chinese converts in Zhejiang were exposed to the gospel while attending one of the mission schools in the province. The missionaries in charge of the schools openly taught the Bible, and gradually the young men and women in their charge began to understand the claims of Jesus Christ.

One of the more successful of the early converts was a man named Xiang Yinggui, who came from a long line of Confucian scholars. Despite his great knowledge, Xiang felt empty inside and knew there must be more to life. From his youth he had dutifully attended temples, but bowing down and sacrificing to idols left him feeling unfulfilled.

Xiang entered the mission school at Ningbo in 1854, and for the next few years his understanding of the gospel slowly grew. He later testified:

> God's grace was within my heart, as when the light dawns in the East. Finally, when I understood more clearly, I made the decision to trust in God and be the disciple of Jesus. Just when I was about to believe, my brother also received grace through the Holy Spirit to believe the truth.[4]

When news emerged that Xiang and his brother had become followers of the "foreign doctrine," the strong opposition from their family members and relatives reflected the kinds of struggles many Chinese Christians experienced at the time. Xiang Yinggui wrote:

> When my mother heard that both of us believed, she was greatly incensed, considering that we had taken up with heretical belief and cast away our ancestors. She wept and wailed night and day, and resisted us with all her might. Besides, there were our other relatives, greater and lesser uncles, cousins, and our neighbors, who used their best endeavor to oppose our believing. By the help of God, we two brothers were unchanged in our purpose.[5]

Xiang Yinggui persevered, and later became a key church leader in the Ningbo area, wholeheartedly serving Christ for many years.

Another early disciple in Zhejiang was Xiang Xinsang, better known in the Western world as Stephen Dzing. He was described as:

> an educated man, practicing as a physician, and owning a small house with some land attached, about 12 miles [19 km] south of Ningbo. A thoughtful man by nature, he had sought peace of mind not only upon the principles of Confucius, but also in the rules of Buddhism. Medical help afforded to one of his

*Xiang Xinsang (Stephen Dzing)*

children by a native Roman Catholic had made him acquainted
with their doctrines . . . He soon became a convert, and zealously propagated his new-found faith among his family and
acquaintances.[6]

Over time, Xiang studied the Scriptures and, under the influence of William Russell and Bao Youyi, turned his back on
Catholicism. He was baptized in Ningbo, and "after a full and
clear renunciation of error and protestation of the truth . . .
he joined 35 other Chinese Christians in receiving the Holy
Communion."[7]

Xiang earnestly assisted the missionaries as they evangelized
throughout the district, and he became a zealous student of the
Scriptures.[8]

As time went by, however, the Evangelical missionaries were
disturbed to find that vestiges of Catholicism remained in
their disciple. Russell spent much time trying to purge Xiang
Xinsang's mind of the Catholic doctrines he had formerly

embraced, but the struggle for his doctrinal purity concluded when he failed to recover from an illness in March 1862. Russell wrote: "His death was happy and triumphant; in the closing hours of his life he committed himself with confidence into the hands of that Lord and Savior whom he had so evidently and intelligently loved and so zealously served."[9]

## *A trail of churches*

The zealous Welsh evangelist Griffith John and his wife Margaret were among the first Evangelical missionaries to travel throughout Zhejiang in the 1850s. During their long career in China, the Johns left a trail of thriving believers wherever they traveled, and the same happened when they passed through Zhejiang Province.

The Johns set out from Shanghai in March 1858 and rented a house at Pinghu in northeast Zhejiang. During the summer

*Griffith and Margaret John*

months they spent much time in the town, "preaching daily to excellent congregations. A class was formed of six enquirers, and afterwards a church was established."[10]

The Johns soon fixed their eyes on the famous city of Hangzhou, which Westerners of the day had nicknamed "the Athens of China." There, Griffith and Margaret found a small group of Christian women who had yet to outwardly declare their faith. Customs of the era dictated that a woman should never meet with a man, especially a foreigner. The presence of Margaret, however:

> dispelled all fear, and these good women gladly came forward to make a public confession of their faith in Jesus. When Mrs. John entered the house, an immense crowd followed, and as many as possible crowded into the guest room where she sat. The host and hostess found it impossible to restrain the curiosity of the people . . . Mr. John examined the female candidates, and those whose faith satisfied him were admitted to the church by baptism . . . A service for the men was next conducted in the adjoining room, and five were admitted as members.[11]

## *An epic love story*

Many Christians are aware of the life and impact made by the founder of the China Inland Mission, Hudson Taylor, but not so many are familiar with the story of how he and the woman he loved, Maria Dyer, were forced to endure a long and painful process before they finally came together in marriage.

Zhejiang was the stage for much of Taylor's early ministry in China. He and his friend William Burns lived in boats and traveled along the interconnecting canals and waterways of the province, sharing the gospel with everyone they met. After one meeting, Taylor wrote:

*Hudson and Maria Taylor*

I was preaching the good news of salvation through the finished work of Christ when a middle-aged man stood up and said . . . "I have looked for the truth a long time, as my fathers did before me, but without getting it. I have found no rest in Confucianism, Buddhism or Daoism. But I do find rest in what I have heard here tonight. From now on, I am a believer in Jesus."[12]

The man who was to become what many observers consider the greatest ever missionary to China seems to have been a hopeless romantic in the early years of his career. After his engagement to an English lady failed, Taylor fell into a time of depression just prior to his visit to the port city of Ningbo in 1856. While there, Taylor met the teenaged Maria Dyer, and his interest was piqued. Hudson described Maria in his diary as "a dear sweet creature . . . She is a precious treasure, one of sterling worth and possessed with an untiring zeal for the good of this poor people."[13]

Maria Dyer was born in China to missionary parents, and had come under the influence of Mary Ann Aldersey, who was not only the first female Evangelical missionary to the Orient but is even thought to have been "the first single Western woman to set foot in China."[14] Although Aldersey's life was a beacon of light in the darkness for many years, and she funded a girls' school in Ningbo completely from her personal income, she is most remembered for the spoiling role she played in doing all she could to stop Hudson from marrying Maria.

Taylor wrote a letter to Maria declaring his love for her and his hope that they would be united in marriage. The letter was delivered to Maria's school by a fellow missionary, and the young teacher waited until class was finished for the day before nervously opening the envelope. Maria later wrote: "I read of his attachment to me, and how he believed God had given him that love for me which he felt. I could hardly understand that it was a reality. It seemed that my prayers were indeed answered."[15]

Hudson, however, was devastated when he received her reply. Instead of accepting his offer, Maria wrote: "I must answer your letter as appears to me to be according to God's direction. And it certainly appears to be my duty to decline your proposals."[16]

Taylor's letter had been intercepted by Aldersey, who literally stood over her teenage charge and dictated the response. Aldersey, who was approaching 60 years of age, had been appointed Maria's legal guardian while she was in China, and the young Englishwoman respected her authority.

Aldersey then wrote to Maria's family members in England, doing all she could to spoil Taylor's reputation and to ruin any future chance of a union between them. She told them about the uneducated upstart, and how he had come to China in faith and started wearing local clothing. Most ghastly of all, he had shaved his head and wore a ponytail in keeping with the custom of Chinese men of the day. Many missionaries found Taylor's stance intolerable and humiliating, and they wanted nothing more than to drive him off the mission field and send him back to England as a failure.

Hudson was dejected when he received Maria's letter, but he strongly suspected the words were not her own. He discreetly arranged a secret "interview" in July 1857, where he again declared his love for Maria, this time in the presence of a fellow missionary.

When news got out of the seemingly harmless meeting, the mission community at Ningbo was thrown into an uproar. Aldersey threatened a lawsuit, while missionary William Russell was so outraged he suggested Taylor "ought to be horsewhipped."[17]

The young Hudson Taylor faced a dilemma. He knew he was called to give his life to China, and he was also certain God had shown him that Maria was to be his life partner. When some

*The house where Hudson Taylor lived when he first came to Ningbo in 1856*

missionaries suggested he return to England and complete his education so that he would be worthy of Maria, she firmly opposed this move, saying:

> I would wait if he went home in order to increase his usefulness. But is he to leave his work in order to gain a name for the sake of marrying me? If he loves me more than Jesus he is not worthy of me—if he were to leave the Lord's work for the world's honor, I would have nothing further to do with him.[18]

The fierce opposition to their relationship continued unabated, and Maria found herself practically under house arrest. She was even forbidden to take Communion until she "gave evidence of repentance for the sin" of considering Taylor's advances. The dire episode weighed heavily on Hudson. He was crushed not by his own struggles but by the thought that Maria was being dragged through the mud. In a letter home he wrote: "Maria is charged with being a maniac, being fanatical, being indecent, weak-minded, too easily swayed; too obstinate and everything else bad."[19]

Months passed without the two single missionaries seeing each other. No communication between the pair was possible, and the protagonists believed their plot to destroy the potential union had succeeded. In November 1857, however, a mutual friend decided to take a risk by arranging a secret meeting between the two lovebirds.

It was instantly clear that the forced separation and unhinged opposition had completely failed to dent their love for each other. Hudson and Maria:

> became secretly engaged, and they hugged and kissed and prayed and talked and kissed some more—with no apologies to make. Wrote Taylor: "I was not long engaged without trying to make up for the number of kisses I ought to have had these last few months."[20]

Maria's uncle back in England was confused about the commotion taking place on the other side of the world. Aldersey had barraged him with letters condemning Taylor, but when Maria's uncle asked other ministers for their opinion of Taylor, their overwhelmingly positive endorsements caused him to write to his niece, granting his approval of their union. Hudson Taylor and Maria Dyer were finally married at Ningbo on January 20, 1858.

The newlyweds remained in Zhejiang for three years, before returning to England, where Hudson studied medicine so he could better minister the love of Christ in China. It was during that trip that the Holy Spirit impressed on Taylor the need for a new, different mission organization—one where the workers would be integrated into Chinese culture as much as possible, with a focus on provinces away from the coast where the majority of missionaries were located. The non-denominational China Inland Mission (CIM) was birthed.

When Hudson and Maria finally returned to China in 1866, they were accompanied by their four children and 15 new missionary recruits. After the group encountered much ridicule and scorn from the sophisticated missionaries in Shanghai, Taylor moved its base of operations south to Hangzhou. Many difficult and tragic times ensued, including the death of the couple's beloved daughter Grace, who had contracted meningitis.

At Christmas 1869, Hudson and Maria made the most difficult decision of their lives. Their four eldest children, Herbert, Howard, Samuel and Maria, were to be sent back to England, where they could stay with their grandparents and attend a regular school. On the journey down the Yangtze River to the ship that would take them across the oceans, six-year-old Samuel slipped into a coma after not feeling well for days, and sadly died. In driving rain, Maria and Hudson buried him next to Grace in a small cemetery in Zhejiang.

The tragedy was compounded when the Taylors bade farewell to their three living children at the dock in Shanghai a few days later. Tears streamed down their cheeks as they wept aloud, not knowing if they would ever see them again in this life.

The following summer was especially hot, and Maria, who was again pregnant, fell ill. In July she gave birth to a baby boy, Noel, who survived only a few weeks. A few days later, Maria also went to be with her Lord, at the age of just 33. After enduring the scorn of many just to make it to the altar, Hudson and Maria Taylor had been married for only 12 years.

## *A new focus*

Although devastated and shaken by the death of his much loved wife, Hudson threw himself into his call with renewed determination. Once again he decided to return to England, this time to speak at meetings and mobilize new workers.

After struggling to overcome the tragic events of 1870, Hudson was feeling terribly lonely without his beloved Maria by his side. During the long journey home he got to know one of the passengers, a 27-year-old single missionary, Jennie Faulding. They married after arriving in England, and returned to China together in 1872.

Although Jennie was a very different person from Maria, Hudson loved her, and together the ministry of the CIM flourished and grew. Hudson traveled widely throughout China, and his burden for the evangelization of the world's most populous country boomed out across the Christian world, prompting many to pray earnestly for China's salvation. His clarion calls for more missionaries resounded throughout the Western Church, and a steady flow of recruits gave their lives to reach China for Christ. One of the many

*Hudson and Jennie Taylor*

memorable and stirring quotes to come from Taylor's pen at this time was:

Shall not the eternal interests of one-fifth of our race stir up the deepest sympathies of our nature with the most strenuous effort of our Blood-bought powers? shall not the low wail of helpless, hopeless misery, arising from half the heathen world, pierce our sluggish ear and rouse us, spirit, soul and body, to one mighty, continued, unconquerable effort for China's salvation? That strong in God's strength and in the power of His might, we may snatch the prey from the hand of the mighty; that we may pluck these brands from the everlasting burning, and rescue these captives from the thralldom of sin and Satan; to grace the triumph of our Sovereign King, and to shine forth forever as stars in His diadem.[21]

Taylor launched a plan to recruit 1,000 new missionaries, declaring: "Souls on every hand are perishing for lack of knowledge; more than 1,000 every hour are passing away into death and darkness."[22]

Satan continually battered Hudson Taylor and did all he could to destroy the CIM, but by 1882 the organization had established bases in every province of China. By 1895, three decades after the mission began, the CIM had more than 640 missionaries scattered throughout the length and breadth of the country. Zhejiang always retained a special place in Taylor's heart because of the key role it had played in the early days of the mission.[23]

A century later, Ralph Winter of the US Center for World Mission offered this tribute to the impact of Hudson Taylor's life:

> With only trade school medicine, without any university experience, much less missiological training, and a checkered past in regard to his own individualistic behavior while he was on the field, he was merely one more of the weak things that God uses to confound the wise . . .
>
> God strangely honored him because his gaze was fixed upon the world's least-reached peoples. Hudson Taylor had a divine wind behind him. The Holy Spirit spared him from many pitfalls, and it was his organization, the China Inland Mission . . . that eventually served in one way or another over 6,000 missionaries, predominantly in the interior of China.[24]

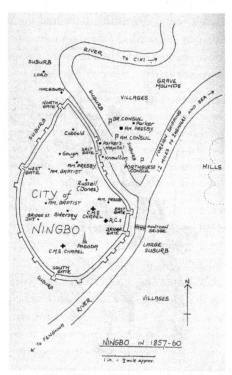

*Ningbo emerged as the hub of Christianity in Zhejiang. This 1860 map shows each church and mission home in the city*

## *A firm foundation*

Because of its status as one of the five "treaty ports" in China at the time, Ningbo remained a key center of mission activity throughout the 1860s. Scotland-born William Parker and his wife arrived in March 1862, in the midst of the Taiping Rebellion. Ningbo was controlled by the rebels at the time and no mission work was possible. That summer, however, the rebels were expelled by British and French troops, and Parker was soon hard at work.

The following year, right when it seemed Parker was beginning to reap from his faithful sowing, he was returning home on horseback one afternoon when he rode across a bridge over one of the narrow canals in the city. Suddenly:

> A stone slab of the bridge gave way, and he was precipitated into the canal, receiving injuries which proved fatal a few days afterwards. This was a heavy blow to the young and still feeble mission, but Ningbo was not left long by our Church without a witness to the truth, for by April 1864 Dr. John Parker was carrying on the work of his lamented brother.[1]

From the beginning, most of the Chinese converts in Zhejiang were instructed by the missionaries not to look for handouts. If a group of local believers needed a chapel or church building, they were expected to pool their resources and trust God to provide. If they wanted to support an evangelist, it was made clear to them that the responsibility was theirs. As a result, the Zhejiang churches were taught to depend upon God and not foreign funding. This established them on a strong foundation, and when storms of persecution later swept in—including ultimately the removal of all foreigners from China—the body of Christ in Zhejiang stood firm and was able to survive the onslaught.

Looking back, the Zhejiang missionaries' insistence that local believers lead and fund the work of the gospel undoubtedly played a large role in bringing about the situation we have today, where the province has the highest percentage of Christians of any province in China. A Zhejiang missionary,

John Butler, expounded on the benefits of weaning the local churches from the dependency on outside funding:

> When the multitude that followed our Lord found that there was no worldly advantage to be gained from connection with Him, but rather that discipleship involved self-denial, hardship and persecution, many of them followed no more with Him. When the pressure of self-support is brought to bear upon a congregation of converts from heathenism, it often results in some being offended and falling away. But it just as often results in bringing to light cases of earnestness, zeal and liberality far beyond your expectations.[2]

The foundation that was laid during the first 20 years of Evangelical endeavor in Zhejiang began to reap rewards in the 1870s. An 1876 report noted:

> Nine years ago . . . there was not one Christian in Shaoxing; but the gospel was preached, and, as a result, we now have a church of 70 Christian disciples, besides about 30 enquirers in whom we have hope. Two other missionaries in the same city have also about 20 converts each. In the Fenghua District, Mr. Crombie has about 50 converts, and here in Hangzhou we have over 40.[3]

## *Trophies of grace*

One of the early church members in Ningbo was a believer named Chu who had fallen into the hands of bandits. The evil men branded him on his cheek and forehead, forever marking him as one of their own. The branding made escape almost impossible, as imperial soldiers were accustomed to behead anyone they came across who was branded in this manner.

When the Ningbo church found out what had happened to Chu they began praying earnestly for him every day. Then:

To their joy and amazement one morning he walked into their meeting, but so altered as to be scarcely recognizable. He told a marvelous tale of God's preserving care, and of the preciousness he had found in the Word of God as his only companion and comfort. He read it night and morning with the feeling that it might be the last time he would be permitted to open his precious New Testament. The deep scars on his face were produced partly by the branding, and partly by the surgical operations he underwent for the removal of characters which might have cost him his life.[4]

Chu went on to become one of the leaders of the body of Christ in Ningbo. He led many people to the Lord Jesus Christ with his gentle and persuasive preaching style.

Another pastor, Xiang Xiaoyong of Shaoxing, recalled how he was influenced to become a Christian as he traveled throughout Zhejiang:

I heard an old man from the country speaking very earnestly. This, together with the sight of so many natives worshipping and believing, much impressed me. On the return journey I saw many believers . . . several of whom exhorted me. I said to myself, "All of these people are believers; they are all intelligent persons; shall I be left behind?"

And again, I was much struck by seeing foreigners frequently on their knees, praying; though, for the life of me, I could not make out at the time what they were doing; at last I concluded that they must be worshipping the God whom they exhorted us to worship . . . Thus I was persuaded. I determined to give myself to Jesus, and He received me.[5]

## *George and Grace Stott*

As Christian influence began to grow throughout the 1870s, the missionaries and Chinese church leaders saw an explosion of interest in the gospel. One of the most prominent missionaries

*George and Grace Stott were instrumental in bringing the gospel to Wenzhou, which today is nicknamed "the Jerusalem of China" due to its massive Christian community*

was a Scottish amputee, George Stott, who had lost one of his legs as a teenager. His wife Grace later shared that story:

> Mr. Stott had been brought up in farm work, but when he was about 19 years of age he slipped on the road and knocked his knee against a stone. This simple accident resulted in white swelling, which, two years later, necessitated the amputation of his left leg. For nine months he lay a helpless invalid, and it was during this time that the Lord graciously saved his soul. He had previously been careless and indifferent to the love of God in Christ Jesus, but now, in his helpless condition, and what seemed his ruined future, how precious that love became! After his recovery he began to teach in a school, and had been thus employed several years when he first heard of China's needs.[6]

Most mission societies of the era would not consider an amputee for service on the mission field, but Hudson Taylor was impressed by Stott. When Taylor asked George why he, with only one leg, should consider going to China, Stott dryly answered, "I do not see those with two legs going, so I must."

After being fitted with a new artificial leg, George Stott sailed for China in November 1867. Soon after arriving in Wenzhou, he encountered problems with the locals, who did not want a foreigner residing in their city. Several times Stott agreed to rent a house, only for the landlord to change his mind under pressure from the community.

After finally finding a wealthy man who was bold enough to go through with the deal, Stott quietly moved in, but by the next morning news had spread and an angry mob assembled, determined to drive the missionary out of the house and the city. As the townspeople smashed down the fence around the property, Stott courageously detached his artificial leg and came out to calmly address them, saying:

> "You see I am a lame man. If I wanted to run from you I could not. If you kill me you will, perhaps, get into trouble. If you let me alone you will find I shall do no harm; anyhow, I have come and mean to stay." They were taken aback by his quiet, strong words, and contenting themselves by throwing a few stones, they dispersed and left him in peace.[7]

After establishing a free school for boys in the city, Stott felt that everything was going well, until one day he turned up to find an empty classroom. A rumor had circulated throughout the city that the missionary was intending to kill the boys and use their hearts and livers for medicine, and for months the local people stayed far away from the school. George Stott was not the kind of person to give up, however. Full of determination and faith, he:

> limped from one village to another, living in abandoned temples and pagodas. He labored for the Lord unceasingly, preaching the

gospel of Christ. He bore shame and scorn and never gave up . . . After a while, he thought the village people might be simpler and more open to the gospel. When he arrived at a village, he caused quite a stir because the villagers had never seen a foreigner before. When he began to sing, the people stopped whatever they were doing and listened. Then Stott would preach the gospel. Without warning, the children pelted him with stones. He fled to another village, where he met with the same reception.[8]

The first years of Evangelical Christianity in Wenzhou had been anything but smooth sailing, and nobody imagined the great plans God had that would one day turn the city into a power-house of Christianity in Asia.

In 1870 Stott traveled to Scotland to marry Grace Ciggie of Glasgow, and the newlyweds returned to Wenzhou. Western women were rarely seen in China in those days, but George noticed that when he visited places with his wife, many wonderful opportunities arose that didn't occur when he traveled alone. In 1875 he wrote:

I took my dear wife with me into the country on a visiting and preaching tour. Crowds came running from every direction to see her (they had seen me often), and their curiosity was highly excited . . . I had many hundreds to hear me at some places, and Mrs. Stott spoke to many women. Some listened attentively, and asked intelligent questions as to how they were to serve the living and true God.[9]

When the Stotts stayed at the rural home of one of their church members, 11 people joined the family in prayer each morning and evening. One by one the villagers threw away their idols and trusted in Christ alone. On the day the Stotts returned to Wenzhou, an elderly woman grabbed their hands and declared:

Oh, how kind of Jesus to send you here to tell us of salvation! We knew nothing of His precious Name until you taught us. I

41

love to hear you speak; but my poor eyes cannot see you, but as a shadow . . . I was not blind the first time you came here, some years ago; but I did not love the doctrine or know Jesus then, and did not care to look at you. Now I love the doctrine and love you for bringing it, but I cannot see your face no matter how I try; but I will feel your hands.[10]

## *Overcomers for Christ*

As the number of Christians increased throughout the province, incidents of persecution also rose. When discovered, converts were often beaten by family members, who felt they had brought disgrace on their ancestors by embracing the "foreign doctrine." One young man, a dwarf, was prohibited from attending Sunday services by his father-in-law and uncle, and their friends.

Undeterred, the man found a way to escape their clutches and attend the weekday meetings. His relatives beat him for this, then bound him with ropes and cast him out of the family home. When they took his property and told him he could no longer have his wife, he replied: "No matter; when my father and my mother forsake me, then the Lord will take me up." After being invited to stay in a room connected to the chapel, the young man said, "Now I am blessed. I am where I can hear the truth continually; they have frustrated their own ends."

His family would not give up, however, and made one last attempt to "bring him to his right mind." A report in 1875 noted:

His father-in-law, uncle, brother-in-law, and even his own wife came to him, and with tears besought him to change his mind. It was a trying moment, and those who were watching him trembled for the result; but grace triumphed, and for some time he has been left in peace. Already his consistent conduct is having its result, and the brother-in-law who beat and opposed him is now inquiring for himself about the gospel which he previously hated.[11]

While Christian influence in Zhejiang was still minimal, the Christians were treated as a curiosity by the general population. When fellowships of wholehearted believers sprang up in hundreds of locations throughout the province, however, trouble soon followed. Many reports of cruel persecution came in, but most believers maintained their faith in spite of overwhelming pressure. Even non-Christian landlords who had rented homes to the missionaries were tortured by enraged judges. One landlord was "compelled to kneel on red-hot iron chains until the flesh was burned to the bone, after which the judge beat him so cruelly that for a time no hope was entertained of his life."[12]

At Shaoxing—a city once nicknamed "the Ephesus of China" due to its prominent idol industry—missionary James Meadows visited a new believer who had already experienced much abuse at the hands of his relatives and neighbors. Meadows remarked:

> His father was outraged, and determined to prevent him having anything to do with the hated religion of Jesus . . . The father had a long heavy chain forged, and bought a big stone with holes for the chain . . . He lifted up his hands to heaven, and declared that he would either discard his son, or sell him to the foreigners, or he should be chained in front of the house as one who was not fit to roam at large, seeing he was bewitched by the religion of the red-haired men. The mother-in-law declared her intention to commit suicide; the wife determined she would no longer be his wife; and the clan, or tribe, resolved to cast him out of their midst.[13]

Despite the enormous pressure to recant, this man remained faithful, and a short time later was publicly baptized into the body of Christ. He, and many others like him, became key living stones in the foundation of the Church in Zhejiang. Later generations of believers followed their shining examples and remained faithful even unto death.

## *Y. T. Zia, a man after God's heart*

One of the key early church leaders in Zhejiang Province was Zia Ying Tong (better known in English as Y. T. Zia), who was born into a poor family at Ningbo in 1825. His father died when he was three years old, and his brother also passed away a few years later. Zia's mother carried on, lovingly finding a way to provide for her children.

By the time Zia was a teenager he had followed his ancestors into idolatry, and regularly visited the temples to pay homage. One day he heard that a missionary, William Martin, had opened the doors of the chapel and was welcoming people to come and ask him questions about Christianity. Zia was curious, and reckoned he had more than a hundred questions

*Y. T. Zia in later years*

he wanted to pose to the foreigner. Martin patiently answered all of Zia's questions, and by the end of their time together the young man was convinced that Christianity was the true religion. In time he surrendered his life to Jesus and was baptized in 1855.

For a year Zia was employed as a teacher at Mary Ann Aldersey's school for girls, and although he did a good job, his heart yearned to roam the countryside sharing the gospel with those who had never heard it. He moved with his young wife to a region 40 miles (65 km) northwest of Ningbo, where:

> he labored most faithfully and successfully for about three years, preaching in tea-shops, rest-houses, or wherever he could get a hearing. At night a few interested ones gathered at his home, and they often talked about the gospel until far into the night. Not a single village in the whole region was omitted in this faithful evangel.[14]

Zia expanded his ministry of evangelism throughout the Zhejiang countryside, and churches grew in size and grace wherever he went. When the Taiping rebels took control of Ningbo in 1861, Zia continued preaching in the chapel until they captured him and his brother and marched them off to their camp.

During the time they spent in the rebel camp, the brothers were subjected to cruel treatment and hardships, but what pained Y. T. Zia the most was the open debauchery and idolatry of the rebels, even though they professed to worship the one true God. He was convinced that to participate in their worship would be an act of idolatry, so he decided to have nothing to do with it. His decision was not a light one, for every day the rebels would give a roll call, and if any of their captives refused to bow down to the idols they would be summarily executed on the spot. Zia realized his stand was likely to cost him his life.

For the next two days Zia managed to slip away before the roll call, and was not required to worship the spirits. On the third evening he was in deep agony of soul and could not sleep, as he realized it was only a matter of time before the rebels called his name or discovered he had eluded them. After struggling in prayer for many hours, the peace of the Holy Spirit flooded Zia's heart, and he knew that whether he lived or died, he would not compromise.

At ten o'clock that night, as he walked around the perimeter of the camp, Y. T. Zia heard his name being called. He hurried toward the sound, and:

> was met by two missionaries who had sought for him daily since his capture, and were making one last effort before giving up the search. They procured the release of Zia and his brother and restored them to their waiting friends . . . A band of Christians had not ceased praying for him day and night, and it was a direct answer to prayer . . . From this point forward his life was even more fully consecrated than before.[15]

In 1864 Zia became the first ordained Presbyterian minister in China. His first pastorate was a congregation of 70 members at Sanbo to the northwest of Ningbo. For the next 13 years he faithfully led the flock, without neglecting his call to win unbelievers to Christ. He often walked for days over mountains and through valleys, searching for lost sheep to bring into God's fold, and hundreds of sinners were saved. He was often accompanied on those journeys by his sons, who gained a firsthand education in how to serve God.

Everywhere he went, Zia was respected as a man of impeccable integrity. He constantly amazed shopkeepers by returning small amounts of cash they had overpaid to him, and an incident at his mother's funeral illustrates the hatred he had for idolatry. God had rescued Zia from that empty life, and it pained him to think anyone might associate him with idolatry ever again. At the funeral service:

> when an ode to the departed spirit was read which referred to the members of the family as kneeling, he said in a loud, clear voice, "Zia Ying Tong and his sons are not kneeling!" When his brother and friends expostulated with him for making unnecessary disturbance, since all could see he was not kneeling, he replied, "But there may have been a blind man in the audience."[16]

Later in life, regular asthma attacks slowed Zia down and he was compelled to reduce his travels. He remained at Ningbo, teaching the local believers and attending to church matters.

On May 12, 1895, the 70-year-old beloved pastor finished his earthly service with the words "Thank God, thank God" on his lips.

One of the deepest desires of Y. T. Zia's life was to see his three sons grow up to serve the Lord with all their hearts. God granted him this desire, and the gospel was handed down to the next generation. His first son became an elder in the church and assisted with evangelistic work. The second was a pastor, and his youngest son graduated from Bible school and became a preacher even while his father was still living.

## A decade of breakthroughs

As the 1870s wound down, the living God looked down from heaven upon Zhejiang and saw a strong and growing Church forming throughout the province. The decade had witnessed many breakthroughs for the gospel, and the body of Christ had increased in grace and in number.

One example of encouraging growth occurred in the mountainous village of Zhuji, which is now a city in its own right, located 40 miles (65 km) south of Hangzhou. One day in the

1870s, a man from Zhuji visited Hangzhou and walked past the chapel, which was not being used at the time. He caught sight of the words "Holy Religion of Jesus" on a sign above the door and asked the neighbors what the word "Jesus" meant. They directed him to the mission home in the city, and over time this inquisitive man became a sincere follower of Christ. He carried the gospel to his native village, and from that humble beginning the church in Zhuji grew to more than 500 baptized believers.

The growth of the gospel in Zhejiang was not evenly spread, however. At Huangyan the missionary lamented at having baptized just two converts after nine years, one of whom died, while the other seldom attended the services. At this low ebb, the Holy Spirit began to move in Huangyan, even though the missionary was a cessationist, believing that miracles no longer occurred.

Despite the missionary's lack of faith, before long 25 people at Huangyan had placed their trust in Christ. The startling breakthrough occurred after a poor visiting evangelist named Xiang Yongkou read in the Scriptures that Jesus healed the sick when He was on the earth. He concluded that if people prayed in faith, God would continue to make them well, and so he began a ministry of healing. The astonished missionary conceded:

> This soon spread, and others called these men to pray for their sick folk, and they recovered. Others tried the same plan with a like result. Now the chapel is too small to hold the people that attend, and we are trying to get a more suitable one.[17]

Evangelist Xiang continued praying for the sick and seeing them healed for many years. A missionary at Taizhou reported:

> Xiang Yongkou was the first person converted in the Prefecture of Taizhou, and was baptized in April 1869 . . . So full was

Yongkou of the new truth he had received that he was compelled to tell it to others . . . The secret of his success seems to be his implicit faith in prayer. Tell him that God does not answer prayer, and he will soon give you instances of God having answered his prayers.

He has prayed over the sick, taking James 5:15 literally. Sometimes he has called others to go with him, and sometimes he has gone alone, and the sick have recovered. I visited those who have been healed in their homes, and heard from their own lips how they began to recover from the time he prayed by their bedside. Some were cases of dysentery, where there seemed no human hope of recovery, others of continued fever, etc. At one place several were raised up this way, and it led to the conversion of some; and, as a result, an idol temple has been turned into a chapel, and over 50 persons have been baptized.[18]

In the 1870s a number of remarkable statements of faith were uttered by missionaries and Chinese believers about the future blessing God would bring to Zhejiang. The men and women who spoke these prophetic utterances did so with few visible signs of encouragement, yet they somehow caught a glimpse of a far-off day when masses of people in Zhejiang would worship the Lord Jesus Christ. In a letter written in November 1878, James Meadows told of four new converts, before declaring:

We thank God for these four souls, and for eight other candidates at the same place. But what are four among so many? Oh, that we could write to you and our friends at home of four thousand or even four hundred receiving the gospel at once! Well, if the Lord Jesus could make five loaves and two small fishes go so far among 5,000 persons, satisfying their hunger and making them to feel comfortable and happy, truly He can make even four souls of much use, and fit them to accomplish much in His blessed kingdom and service.

We long as much for quality as we do for quantity. If we had the former, in the shape of a deeper work of grace in all our hearts, the latter would then be its natural outcome; and we would see the lame man leap as the deer, and hear the tongue of the dumb sing. We would then see the waters break out in the wilderness, and streams in the desert. May God hasten this happy day![19]

# *1880s*

*A gathering of Chinese pastors and missionaries from Wenzhou and Pingyang in the 1880s*

## *Mounting opposition*

The new decade commenced with fresh hopes that the gospel would rapidly advance among the masses of Zhejiang. Although the overwhelming majority of people in the province had never heard the Name of Jesus Christ, a steady expansion of the work had taken place throughout the 1870s. A survey of Evangelical churches in Zhejiang in 1880 found there to be 69 foreign missionaries, 25 native pastors, 50 churches and a total of 2,051 believers throughout the province.[1]

One of the chief reasons for this newfound confidence was the way that God had raised up gifted Chinese men to lead the Church in the province. In 1882 the CIM published a letter written by Wen Jiseng, who was the Chinese pastor at

Fenghua in northern Zhejiang. In his letter, which was broadly addressed to Christians in Britain, Wen wrote:

> I am now going to write a few words to the brethren in your honorable country, but they must not be looked upon as words of exhortation, because I am one of the Lord's unworthy disciples and I do not understand the truth well . . . You English disciples cannot but be more advanced than we Chinese are, because you have had God's truth for so many generations, and have learned it from your childhood, while we have many customs and plans which lead us to trust in our own righteousness; so first I want to ask you to pray for us; to pray God to pour out His Spirit as at Pentecost, and to influence us . . .
>
> I ought also to thank you foreign brethren because you brought the gospel to us. If you had not brought it we would still be in darkness. There are many of you who labor for us; there are many of you who give much money; there are many of you who pray earnestly for us; and again there are those who wish to come to China to preach the gospel that many Chinese may be saved. For all this I thank you . . .
>
> Among the hills near Fenghua is a place where many foreigners visit a waterfall. Once, one of the men of this place said to me, "The foreigners continually come to these hills to look for precious things." I said, "No, not to seek precious things, but to seek a cool retreat. The foreigners have one very precious thing which they are willing to give to you." He asked, "What thing?" and I replied, "It is the blood of Jesus Christ." I then preached the truth of the cross to him, and he listened for a long time.[2]

An expected challenge to the Evangelical churches emerged in the 1880s. The Roman Catholics had been established in Zhejiang for almost three centuries, and were scattered throughout the province. The two groups had previously left one another alone, but by the late 1880s Evangelicals were increasingly frustrated at Catholic interference in their activities. One missionary complained:

> The Romanish Church is manifesting unwanted activity in central and western Zhejiang, in seeking to proselytize native Christians of the Protestant faith. They diligently visit the houses of the converts, and argue, offering many substantial rewards in return for adherence to the Catholic faith. The priests do not hesitate to add falsehood to argument.[3]

Although the first recorded martyrdom of an Evangelical Christian in Zhejiang occurred when Walter Lowrie was killed in 1847, many Chinese believers had faced years of excruciating hardship and persecution from their families and communities. To most Chinese, becoming a Christian was an act of betrayal, as many considered Christianity to be a tool of Western imperialism, a perception which lingers to some degree to the present day.

In the same way that precious pearls are created by constant friction, the body of Christ in Zhejiang was not destroyed by the hardships it encountered, but rather through these setbacks developed stronger character and unity, resulting in widespread growth throughout the province in the 1880s. Testimonies emerged from many parts of Zhejiang, telling of individuals who had experienced the life-changing grace of the Lord Jesus Christ.

Most persecutions against Zhejiang's Christians were never documented, but a few accounts—representative of many more like them—trickled in from the field. When one Christian man in 1886 refused to worship the village idols or contribute to the local heathen festivities, the men of the community seized him. They then:

> strung him up to a beam, and his right ear and ponytail were cut off, while his life was threatened unless he rejected the doctrines

of Jesus. He stood firm; his ear was healed by a medical missionary at Hangzhou, and he is still worshipping and witnessing for Jesus to his countrymen.[4]

## *Mrs. Liu and the Wenzhou Church*

In the twenty-first century Wenzhou is famous for being "the Jerusalem of China" and thousands of churches dominate the skyline, but in the 1880s the Wenzhou Church was still taking its first tiny steps of faith. One woman named Liu was widowed at the age of 29, and was left to fend for herself and her baby son, with no family to help take care of them. She struggled terribly, and was barely able to produce enough food to stay alive. In her desperation Liu sought spiritual help from all the idols

*Mrs. Liu with her Christian children and grandchildren*

she could find. However, the more lifeless forms she prostrated herself before, the emptier she felt inside.

One day a Christian firewood seller visited Liu's village, and told her and a neighbor about the living God who could forgive their sins and make their lives worth living. Each time the Christian visited he seemed full of life and joy, and both Liu and her neighbor opened their hearts and believed in Jesus.

As she surrendered herself to the mercies of God, Liu found that her skill as an embroiderer became sought after, and she was now better able to make ends meet. Moreover, a great spiritual hunger arose in the hearts of the two new believers, and they longed to learn all they could from the Bible. Missionary Grace Stott regularly visited and held Bible classes in their homes.

After a time, the Holy Spirit seized control of Liu's heart in such a powerful way that the formerly shy single mother began to boldly proclaim the gospel throughout the city. Stott wrote about Liu's unquenchable zeal, saying:

> She went about the city, entering every open door to tell of Christ. She voluntarily gave up her work one day a week to accompany me in visiting the women. Often have tears of joy come to my eyes when I have heard her declare to 30 or 40 women gathered around us in some courtyard that this Jesus, of whom they had just heard, had put away her sin, and could therefore put away theirs. She never wearies in telling them of Christ and His love for lost sinners. This she does solely out of love for Him, for she has never received from us the slightest remuneration . . .
>
> We had long prayed for the conversion of one who could work among the women, and now felt sure our prayers had been answered. Indeed, we could hardly have hoped for one so suitable in every way. Besides being an earnest Christian, she was able to read, was comparatively young, and free.
>
> I asked if she would give up her needlework and devote her whole time to gospel work, and come to live with us that she

might help me to train up the girls in our boarding school. She answered, "I shall be so glad. I have often wished I could do enough work that I might be your servant, and so hear God's Word every day." She refused the offer of money, saying that, if boarded with the girls, she would have enough for all her needs.[5]

A short time later, Mrs. Liu's mother-in-law died and left a considerable property to her. Taking possession of the property, however, required that Liu perform a complex array of ancestral rites and ceremonies. Knowing that such things were an abomination to God, Liu declined the inheritance. Her relatives were amazed, and many who heard about Liu's stance pondered what kind of transformation had taken place in her heart that allowed her to spurn worldly wealth for even greater spiritual riches.

Liu went on to become a "Biblewoman," and a key pillar of the Church in Wenzhou. She led many women to Jesus Christ and was a tireless evangelist, never missing an opportunity to share God's Word with everyone she met.

Liu later moved to Taizhou, where she brought God's light to the inhabitants. Her son grew into a wholehearted disciple of Christ. He married a dedicated believer, and their children also loved Jesus. Liu lived a long and productive life for the kingdom of God. Many people today marvel at the size and influence of Christianity in Wenzhou, but few know that God chose a broken-hearted single mother to be one of His foundation stones of the Church in the city, which today boasts the largest concentration of Christians in China.

## The enemy strikes back in Wenzhou

The Evangelical churches in Wenzhou had begun to flourish, and the hunger for spiritual truth in the city and surrounding areas was more intense than in most other parts of China. With many powerful conversions to Christ occurring throughout the region, it was not long before demonic forces struck back with vengeance against the fledgling churches. An anti-Christian riot erupted in early 1885, with a tearful Grace Stott reporting:

> We have all been burned out of Wenzhou—all our houses, schools, chapels, and everything we possessed, gone and our poor people scattered and troubled on every side . . . My husband, the children, and Dr. MacGowan, who came to help them, were pelted with stones all the way . . .
>
> We feel so deeply thankful that no lives have been lost, that all our other losses seem as nothing. Our greatest sorrow is for our poor people. Many of them are young in the faith. Thirty-nine of them have only this year put on Christ. But He who saved them will keep them.
>
> This is a trial we had never looked for. The Lord was blessing the work. Souls were being saved, and it seemed as if we had nothing to do than sow and reap . . . The devil has not crushed faith and hope out of our hearts. We can still sing and feel thankful that we are counted worthy to suffer for His Name's sake. And we know that He will yet bring good out of this seeming evil, and that which has happened to us shall yet be to the furtherance of the gospel. Gladly would we lay down life itself, if only His Name be glorified.[6]

## Salt and light in Zhejiang

While great things were happening as the gospel spread to many parts of Zhejiang, significant challenges were encountered. One struggle was the high rate of illiteracy among new believers, with one missionary lamenting:

> Not one in ten of our male members could read when he was converted—an unusual state of things for China, but a fact in Wenzhou. I know just one woman out of the 400 members who

could read when she was converted. Thus you see the teaching work among us is very much harder than in some places, because it has to be almost wholly oral.[7]

To help overcome this challenge, God raised up many Christian women who were powerful witnesses to the women and children of Zhejiang. Their vibrant faith in Jesus Christ shone forth through their lives, and even their deaths proved to be opportunities to lead many to repentance. A missionary in Shaoxing, Miss Murray, shared a story about the death of a Christian schoolgirl named De Jing. For weeks De Jing had suffered severe chest pains, and as she gasped for breath, her classmates gathered around her bed. At that point she rallied, and Miss Murray recalled:

> She fixed her beaming eyes on mine, and said, "Oh, I am so happy! Do not weep. You need not be troubled. You must not weep. I am going to heaven. I am inexpressibly happy. I have seen the Lord! I have seen heaven. It is so good; very, very good!"
>
> "Have your sufferings ceased entirely, then?" I asked.
>
> "Only my chest is sore, but that will soon be over. In heaven there will be no pain, no sorrow—no, not the least. Heaven is so good, inexpressibly good! You cannot even imagine how good it is. Oh, I am happy!"
>
> Looking around at us all, she thanked us repeatedly, saying, "You need not weep; you must not weep. We shall meet in heaven. Good-bye, good-bye. Meet me in heaven. Its door is very wide, so that whosoever will may enter if they will only trust in Jesus."
>
> After requesting they sing the hymn Rock of Ages, De Jing gained strength and declared, "It is wholly on account of Jesus' merit that I am pure. I could do nothing to save myself—no, not the least thing."
>
> The next morning De Jing told those gathered around her bed, "When the Lord calls me, I have no pain; when he sends me back, then I have pain. I am going now."[8]

De Jing breathed her last breath and life drained away from her body, but her spirit departed to be with the Savior, whom she loved with all her heart. She left behind a room full of startled friends who would never forget what they had seen and heard. The schoolgirls experienced personal revival, and from that point on they exhibited a new passion for sharing the gospel with others.

An insight into the kind of Church God was raising up throughout Zhejiang can be seen in the fascinating accounts of the questions and answers that occurred when Chinese believers applied to be baptized. At Shaoxing, James Meadows recounted some interesting exchanges with new converts. When he examined a young schoolgirl named Ying Wajing and asked her to explain why she wanted to be baptized, Ying replied, "I am a sinner. My heart is sinful, and what I do is sinful." When pressed as to what she intended to do with her sins, Ying answered, "Jesus can forgive them. He shed His blood on the Cross, that sins might be forgiven."

Finally, when it was pointed out that winter was approaching and the water would be so cold that her friends and relatives might try to dissuade her from going through with the baptism, Ying declared, "I don't fear the coldness of the water, neither will I listen to those who wish me to put off joining the Church. I wish to be baptized at this time, please."[9]

Another teenage girl named Xi had been a handful for the staff at the Shaoxing mission school. She was the worst girl in the school, and regularly flew into violent fits of rage and screamed filthy words, which required her to be forcibly carried out of the classroom by her frustrated teachers. She used to mock the Christian girls at the school, calling them "hypocrites" and vowing that she would never believe.

The Christian girls loved Xi and prayed for her salvation every day. Over time, the Holy Spirit softened her heart and convicted her of sin, righteousness and judgment. One day, the leaders of the school were shocked when the troubled teen announced she was a believer in Jesus Christ and that she desired to be baptized. When questioned, Xi was asked where her sins were now. She replied:

> The Lord Jesus has forgiven them. He came from heaven, became a man, shed His blood, and He has great power and great merit, and can save great sinners . . . I have truly repented and besought the Lord Jesus to forgive me, and He has forgiven me . . . My heart is filled with joy and peace in Jesus; I would like to exhort others to believe in and serve Him.[10]

As the 1880s drew to a close, the China Inland Mission had emerged as a key component in Evangelical missions throughout Zhejiang. By 1883, they reported the following statistics for each region in the province:[11]

Zhejiang, north (based at Hangzhou)—197 baptized since 1866
Zhejiang, north-central (Shaoxing)—187 baptized since 1866
Zhejiang, central (Jinhua)—30 baptized since 1875
Zhejiang, east (Fenghua)—144 baptized since 1866
Zhejiang, southeast (Taizhou)—176 baptized since 1867
Zhejiang, south (Wenzhou)—146 baptized since 1867

By 1883, the CIM had accumulated a total of 880 baptized believers during the 17 years they had worked in Zhejiang. The total gradually increased over the next five years, and stood at 978 baptized believers at the start of 1889.[12]

# 1890s

―――――•◦•――――

## *The kingdom steadily expands*

God's kingdom grew steadily throughout Zhejiang in the 1890s, although the work in Wenzhou suffered a blow when pioneer Scottish missionary George Stott suddenly passed away in 1889, at the age of 54. His wife Grace, after a period of mourning, concluded that God was not finished with her call, and she continued to serve in the city for many years. In May 1890 the leader of the CIM work in Wenzhou noted:

> This has been the most successful year, so far as baptisms and general work is concerned, since the opening of the station over 20 years ago . . . This year, up till now there have been 57

*A group of Christian men at Wenzhou in 1893*

persons received into the Church by baptism, and still there's more to follow! . . . One man from Dongling, formerly a professional boxer, told of the wonderful way in which he was led to the Lord. At first he was bitterly opposed to the doctrine, but like Paul of old, he was arrested in his course, and now goes about the whole countryside in his lawful occupation of cattle-dealer, and at the same time most earnestly preaches Christ to all who care to listen.[1]

## Revival in Taizhou

Although the city and area around Wenzhou had experienced strong growth through the ministry of the Stotts and others, in the 1890s the Taizhou region further north emerged as the powerhouse of Christianity in Zhejiang Province.

Evangelical work had commenced in Taizhou in 1867 when a man heard that Jesus could set people free from opium addiction. He made his way to the mission hospital at Ningbo and underwent successful treatment to liberate him from the drug.

While in the hospital he heard the gospel for the first time. He:

> wrote at once to beg his father to come up and see and hear for himself. The old man came up, and after some time father and son were baptized together . . . Though the son was subjected to violent persecution, he stood firm, and the gospel seed struck root.[2]

In the 1890s the wind of the Holy Spirit blew strongly upon the believers in Taizhou, and their zeal to win the lost resulted in hundreds of conversions every year. Grace Stott recalled one special meeting where the zeal of the Taizhou Christians rubbed off on the Wenzhou believers, causing them to trust God for more salvations:

There had been quite a revival in several of the Taizhou out-stations . . . and [we] longed that we should see like blessing. I asked Mr. Liu if he would give us on Sunday afternoon a little account of the work there; so, instead of separating into our several classes, we all came together to hear what God had been doing in other places. Our hearts warmed as we heard of 147 baptisms in 1892.

In the course of his remarks, Liu said that Wenzhou was considered the first station, both in numbers and spiritual power, while Taizhou was second. When he finished I felt constrained to add a few words. I remarked that Wenzhou had stood first, but could do so no longer. I contrasted our poor 30 baptisms with their 147, and asked who would join me in a week's daily prayer for deeper spiritual power in our own souls, and new life for others. Up went many hands. I asked what we should pray for, and one brother called out, "Seven hundred souls!"

I was taken aback; my poor faith had not risen above 100. I said, "Let us think well before we speak. God is able to give us all we have faith for." Then one dear man called out, "Up with your hands for 300 next year." I pointed out that if each member would win one soul to Christ our numbers would just be doubled, and that seemed very little. So it was settled that as many as possible should meet for prayer every day during the first week of the Chinese year, and that after prayer we should make up several bands, and go in different directions, preaching the glorious gospel, and we expected much blessing.[3]

As the numbers in Table 1 indicate, the CIM's work in Zhejiang flourished under the hand of God's blessing in the 1890s, with annual reports showing a steady cumulative increase in church members.

## Problems abound

In addition to the external pressures on the Church, many internal problems broke out, as often occurs when quick

Table 1  China Inland Mission—Zhejiang in the 1890s

| Year | Baptisms | Church members |
|------|----------|----------------|
| 1890[4] | 154 | 1,097 |
| 1891[5] | 97 | 1,121 |
| 1892[6] | 194 | 1,217 |
| 1893[7] | 236 | 1,518 |
| 1894[8] | 473 | 2,100 |
| 1895[9] | 282 | 1,981 |
| 1897[10] | 801 | 2,980 |
| 1898[11] | 348 | 3,710 |

church growth is experienced. In one short period, five key members of the church in Wenzhou died. These events shook the faith of many new believers, causing Grace Stott to lament that "one family was plunged into sore and continuous persecution. Worst of all, one man fell into open sin, while the pastor forgot his holy calling and gave way to wrath. The pastor's case was particularly sad."[12]

These problems proved to be no more than temporary setbacks in Wenzhou, however, and steady growth soon resumed, with Stott writing in late 1893:

> Our large chapel, which seats 350, has several times been crowded with Christians and inquirers to its utmost capacity, and we are brought face to face with the question of enlarging our borders; either the chapel must be made bigger, or a new one opened outside the South Gate.[13]

As the size and influence of the Church continued to expand throughout Zhejiang, many incidents of persecution broke out against Chinese believers. In 1895 a riot occurred near Pingyang, when local villagers found that the eyes of some of their idols had been scratched out. A feast was held at a temple, where a spirit-priest went into a trance and asked the spirits to reveal who had committed the act.

While under the control of a spirit, the man declared that the deed had been done by followers of the "foreign doctrine" (that is, Christianity). In that particular village there were no Christians at the time, but members of one particular family were known to have inquired into the teaching. They were severely beaten and their goods seized, though they strongly protested their innocence. Notices were circulated throughout the district calling for the extermination of all followers of Jesus.

A few days later an unsuspecting evangelist, Wu Dongfu, passed through the area. A mob accused him of stealing the eyes of the idols. Before Wu had a chance to reply, the enraged villagers beat him, tore his clothes, and were preparing to kill him when a police officer arrived and restored order. Throughout the region at least 18 Christian families had their homes demolished and their possessions looted, leaving them destitute. The attacks continued for some time, causing many believers to flee for their lives.

Undeterred by the violence, a church leader wrote:

> Amid all that has happened, how thankful we are to God that no lives have been lost. We are sure that God has a great purpose in permitting all this trouble to fall upon us. We know that it shall yet all work for lasting blessing to all the Christians involved, as well as being the means of bringing blessing upon our persecutors.[14]

## William Soothill

The Methodists also played a prominent role in the evangelization of Zhejiang in the second half of the nineteenth century. Chief among the Methodist missionary contingent was the brilliant scholar William Soothill from Halifax, England.

*William Soothill traveling by "sedan chair" in the 1890s*

Soothill was pursuing a career in law when his plans were interrupted by a clear call from God to serve on the mission field. He set aside his own goals and determined to follow Christ, no matter where it took him.

After arriving in Wenzhou in 1882, Soothill forged an outstanding career of Christian service. Among his accomplishments, Soothill translated the New Testament into the Wenzhou dialect, and during the 26 years he lived in the city he founded a hospital, a Methodist training college, schools and 200 mission preaching stations. Throughout his career in China, Soothill also challenged some accepted Methodist traditions and exposed them as unbiblical, including the practice of infant baptism. He instead taught the Chinese to dedicate infants to Christ, but to baptize only those adult believers who had demonstrated fruits of repentance and had a solid grasp of the truth.

In October 1884, two years after Soothill commenced his work, an anti-foreign riot broke out because of war between China and France. During the church's Saturday morning prayer meeting, the mission was attacked and set on fire. Soothill and the other believers escaped with their lives, but the Methodist work in Wenzhou suffered a setback until new facilities were built.

At the time of the riots Soothill was engaged to Lucy Farrar, also from Halifax. She was told of the dangerous developments in Zhejiang but was completely unmoved by the news, and set sail for China just weeks later. William and Lucy were married in Shanghai in December 1884, and they enjoyed a long and productive union together for the kingdom of God.

Lucy Soothill proved herself a gifted instrument in God's hand, and she contributed greatly to the work in Wenzhou. On Thursday mornings she led a Bible class for women and girls, and the attendees were so touched by the Spirit of God that before long dozens came each week, bringing their friends and relatives with them.

*Lucy Soothill's Thursday Bible class in Wenzhou*

Blessed with a brilliant mind, William Soothill went on to become President of the Imperial University in Shanxi Province in 1911, and later returned to England where he became Professor of Chinese at Oxford University. However, he was one of those rare individuals with the ability to mix a great academic mind with simple, practical living. Many of his writings dealt with very down-to-earth subjects. On one occasion he exhorted his fellow missionaries not to abandon common sense in their zeal to evangelize the masses of China. Soothill wrote:

> Without common sense, a missionary will neglect his own health and become a burden to his colleagues, his friends, and himself, as did a certain young man, who on being urged to wear a sun-hat and carry an umbrella, smiled serenely, and quoted, "The sun shall not smite thee by day" . . . He is now at home with an enfeebled brain, which, one surmises, can never have been very strong.
>
> Without common sense, a man will change his methods of work so often that his people are quite unable to keep pace with him, or, on the other hand, he may become so conservative that his church will become as lifeless as himself. There are "cranks" at home; there are "cranks" also in the mission field; and few of them succeed in doing enough good work with one hand to cover the harm they do with the other.[15]

On another occasion the always blunt William Soothill shared a humorous yet true story of how local Chinese viewed the missionaries living among them. He wrote:

> On every side there are eyes, many eyes, which apparently see nothing, yet which see everything; and lips which, behind his back, probably nickname him for whatever peculiarity asserts itself. One man of my acquaintance was known as "Old-wait-a-bit," because of his habit of procrastination; another as "Turnip-head" because of his obtuseness, and a few months ago

I read of three others, living in the same compound, who were respectively known as "Bath every day man," "Bath once a week man," and "Never bath at all man."[16]

## *From Buddha to the living God*

Accounts of remarkable Christian conversions continued to roll in from throughout Zhejiang during the 1890s, as the Holy Spirit moved on people's hearts and transformed their lives from darkness to light. One man named Yu Yushan had been an officer in the imperial army during the Taiping Rebellion in the 1850s and 1860s. After the war he joined a strict sect of Buddhism, and traveled around the countryside spreading that doctrine to many people while carrying out his profession as a medical doctor.

Some years later Yu stumbled into a chapel in the city of Jinhua. For one year he attended almost every service, and gradually the light of God's truth dawned in his heart. He surrendered his life to Jesus Christ and was baptized in 1876.

A few months after his conversion, Yu fell ill and was confined to bed. During that time he took stock of his life, and God called him to serve in the neighboring province of Jiangxi, where he had spent much time formerly spreading Buddhist teachings. After summoning missionary A. W. Douthwaite to his bedside, Yu said: "I have led hundreds on the wrong road, and now I want to lead them to the way of truth. Let me go. I ask no wages, nor do I want any of your money. I only want to serve Jesus."[17]

Yu Yushan went out as promised, sharing the salvation of Jesus Christ with as many people as would listen. A year later the missionaries followed in his trail. They baptized 15 of Yu's converts in Taiyang village, and formed a church at another town, which grew to more than 70 members.

Yu Yushan passed into the presence of his Lord and Savior a few years later, but the former Buddhist left behind much good fruit for the kingdom of God.

## *Honoring a much loved missionary*

Of all the foreign missionaries who served in Zhejiang in the nineteenth century, perhaps none was more deeply loved than Grace Stott. Grace and her husband George had arrived in the province after their marriage in 1870, and their hard work and loving, truthful manner soon won the hearts of the Chinese. Grace was especially held in high regard by the women and girls of the city, whom she selflessly served for many years.

In 1888 the Stotts returned to Britain on furlough, but George's health took a turn for the worse. For more than a

*The huge banner lovingly presented to Grace Stott on her fiftieth birthday*

year he struggled to regain his strength, but God wanted him in heaven, and he entered into the glorious presence of Jesus Christ in April 1889. The doctor who was with Stott in his last moments said:

> With every moment's respite from pain he collected his little strength to give forth some word of testimony that the Lord was near, and doubt and fear far away. "It is only the poor body that is suffering," he said; "the soul is happy." Early in the evening he said, "I bless God that 30 years ago He washed me from my sins in His precious blood, and now the sun is shining without a cloud"; and thus with unfaltering faith, and with unwavering hope, he went down into the valley.[18]

After the death of her beloved husband, most people assumed Grace would remain in Britain and lead a quiet life. Instead, she returned to Wenzhou and threw herself into the work with great vigor.

In 1896 the local Christians decided to honor Grace Stott by presenting her with a massive banner on the occasion of her fiftieth birthday. The centerpiece of the banner was a summary of her service to the people of Wenzhou. The English translation reads:

> Mrs. Stott and her husband were the first to come to Wenzhou to preach the holy doctrine of Jesus. When they had newly come, and the gospel had not yet been preached abroad, they were very badly treated by some, who, without any reason whatever, maligned them in every way possible—all which they bore most patiently.
>
> Afterwards, trusting in God's help, they were able to reach the country districts with the gospel . . .
>
> Mr. Stott was called home to heaven; but Mrs. Stott, understanding the mind of the Lord, and in accordance with her husband's desire, again returned . . . While in Wenzhou she set herself to teach the Church members and to feed them with

spiritual food . . . Now in Wenzhou, the ten counties, and all the districts round about, there are many white-haired old men, besides young men, and numbers of women who have all heard the gospel and received her instruction . . .

Today we celebrate her birthday, and have prepared a banner to present to her . . . During these couple of decades great grace has come to us from God. We congratulate her on her birthday, and pray that from today she may have long life.[19]

The following year, Grace Stott wrote an excellent book, *Twenty-Six Years of Missionary Work in China*. The last page of the book aptly summed up the service she and her late husband had performed for the kingdom of God in Wenzhou:

The dark places of the earth are still full of the habitations of cruelty; and yet the missionary's life is one of surpassing joy, for who has ever tasted a delight more intense than that of seeing souls born into the kingdom, and perhaps no country has given larger results for the amount of labor bestowed than China.

It is true that as a nation the people are dirty, treacherous and in many instances cruel; but while they have these and other unlovely national characteristics, I can bear testimony to a warmth of devotion, fidelity, and patient endurance, not exceeded by any country . . . I still hope to spend my remaining years in their midst.[20]

Grace continued to serve in Wenzhou until 1909, when at the age of 63 she retired to Toronto, Canada. She had served in China for 20 years after her husband's death, and 39 years overall.

More than a century has elapsed, but the godly legacy of the Stotts' service in Wenzhou can still be seen. The oldest church in the city, the Chengxi Christian Church, still stands as a testimony to their work long ago. Of greater significance than the building, however, are the millions of consecrated Christians throughout Wenzhou City and the surrounding areas. Today, as many as 30 percent of the population of Wenzhou profess faith in Jesus Christ.[21]

# *1900s*

---

## *The Boxer Rebellion in Zhejiang*

Overall, Zhejiang suffered less Boxer persecution in 1900 than did China's northern provinces, but while most of the missionaries made it to the safety of the coast, many Chinese believers suffered loss of property and a few were killed.

The Christians in Wenzhou reportedly faced "fierce and bitter persecution. One evangelist was murdered, and others suffered serious injuries, as well as loss of house and home."[1] Meanwhile, in and around the large city of Ningbo:

> over 400 families of Christians and inquirers suffered property loss, many being stripped of all their possessions. Their lives were threatened, and dozens of them lived in mountain caves to escape violence. Some died from the fright and hardship of those months, but only one was actually killed.[2]

A Christian man named Sai Enba was over 60 years old at the time of the Boxer attacks. He was a preacher and a man of prayer. The Boxers threatened Sai with death, and when he attempted to escape down the river he found the way blocked. That evening, one of the Boxer chiefs went into a demonic trance and declared that the spirits demanded a human sacrifice, so:

> They went and took old Sai Enba. They carried him to a quiet temple, and, first of all, tried to make him worship the idols. This he refused to do, and they said he must die. He asked time for prayer; but before he had finished they began cutting at his neck with their blunt swords. The murderers were afterwards heard to say that he was still praying when his head was half severed from his body.[3]

## Missionary martyrs

Although most Christians in Zhejiang survived the Boxer onslaught with their lives intact, a group of foreign missionaries located far inland were unable to flee. Their courageous testimonies were an inspiration to Christians throughout the province and around the world.

The city of Quzhou is located in western Zhejiang, approximately 62 miles (100 km) from the border with Jiangxi Province. The CIM commenced work there in 1875, and by the dawn of the twentieth century a small church had been established. In the summer of 1900, Quzhou was home to three single female missionaries plus the Thompson family—consisting of David and Agnes Thompson and their two sons, Edwin (six) and Sidney (two).

David Thompson was born in Scotland in 1854. He met Christ at the age of 19 and sailed for China when he was 26. In

*David and Agnes Thompson and their two sons*
*were martyred for Christ in 1900*

1885 he married Agnes Dowman, and later moved to Quzhou where the couple operated a medical dispensary and shared the gospel with thousands of people. Every patient received a gospel tract, and all who wanted to know more about Jesus were visited by a local Chinese evangelist. After six years of hard work and perseverance, the Thompsons had baptized 62 believers.

Agnes was busy raising her two boys, but she also led a twice-weekly meeting attended by 80 women. When news of the Boxer atrocities in other parts of China reached Quzhou, the missionaries considered fleeing for the coast, before deciding it was safer to remain where they were. On July 20, the day before his death, David Thompson wrote:

> I know not what to say or think; everything up here is growing worse. There are thousands of people taking refuge in the city, and the rebels are gathering now in a body . . . We hear all kinds of evil reports, which make us fear, but by His grace we are able to rise above all, and take hold of our God and Savior. As yet we do not see our way clear to move, for if we leave without a very strong escort we shall be robbed; so we will just "stand still and see the salvation of God." Pray for us . . . Now I will close; and God, our Father, take care of us, or *take* us. His will be done.[4]

The local magistrate in Quzhou, a man named Wu, sincerely assured the missionaries that he would protect them, but on July 21 a mob of enraged locals seized the magistrate, along with his family members and servants, and slaughtered them—31 people in all. That morning, the mission home was attacked by a similar crowd of frenzied people. The Thompsons escaped, but when they raced to the military official's residence for protection they were rejected. With their hopes dashed, the Thompson family:

turned away, sick at heart, to face the cruel mob awaiting them. These, taking their cue from the officials, at once rushed upon Mr. Thompson, dragged him out on the street . . . and stabbed him to death with knives and tridents, his body being covered with wounds. One of the children was then killed in the same way, and the mother pleaded in vain for the life of her second child. The response of the mob was to dash the child on the hard stones, and stab him to death before her eyes, and then she herself was cruelly murdered.[5]

Josephine Desmond was born in West Newton, Massachusetts, in 1867. Her parents were staunch Catholic immigrants from Ireland. While attending a Christian school, Josephine entered into a personal relationship with Jesus Christ. She received a call to missions while attending the Moody Bible Institute in Chicago and, after serving two years as a missionary among a Native American tribe in South Dakota, Desmond applied to join the CIM.

*Josephine Desmond*

She finally departed for China in 1898 and was stationed in remote western Zhejiang Province. In one of her last letters, dated June 6, 1900, Desmond wrote:

> I have been to several of the outstations this spring . . . The people came in crowds and listened well. In one place an old woman believed from the first and stayed with us until she had learned a prayer. It is such a joy to find the "other sheep" in these out-of-the-way places.[6]

The 33-year-old Josephine Desmond was slaughtered alongside the Thompsons on the streets of Quzhou on July 21, 1900. She had served in China for just 18 months.

Etta Manchester was born into a God-fearing family at Edmeston, New York, in 1871. The process of knowing Christ was a gradual one for Etta. It wasn't until she was 19 that she definitely knew she had passed from spiritual death to life.

*Etta Manchester and Edith Sherwood*

The only truly worthwhile career Etta could think of pursuing was one spent proclaiming the gospel among people who had never heard it before. She applied to the CIM, and ultimately sailed for China in 1895, ending up in the town of Quzhou. Manchester was the type of person who made friends easily, and it was said of her:

> She loved the people, and, having got on well with the language, constantly spent weeks itinerating from village to village. Many women were brought to Christ, and there were many inquirers, baptisms, and great encouragement in the work all around.[7]

In the spring of 1900, Etta received a letter telling of her father's failing health, and she was making plans to return to America when the Boxer attacks commenced.

Edith Sherwood was born in England in 1854, and was 17 years older than Etta Manchester. From the start of her life Edith seemed to love the Lord with all her heart, mind and strength, and as a schoolgirl she actively shared her faith with others. After leaving school, she worked among the sick and poor in north London, before joining the Thompsons at their west Zhejiang mission in 1893.

Although she commenced her missionary career at the relatively late age of nearly 40, Sherwood played a key role at Quzhou. She decided it was disadvantageous for missionaries to live in walled compounds separated from the people they had come to reach, so she rented a small house in the middle of a busy neighborhood:

> and as she looked out upon these from her balcony, she prayed and longed for the salvation of the people. She visited freely among them, and was always well received, and for them she was called to lay down her life.[8]

Etta Manchester and Edith Sherwood lived in the north of Quzhou. At about noon on July 21, a mob suddenly invaded their home, and the intruders began to plunder whatever they could lay their hands on. The women tried to escape but were discovered and severely wounded. Etta and Edith somehow managed to pull themselves up and hid on a neighbor's property for the next two days. Under intense pressure, the neighbors finally decided they could not sacrifice their lives to protect the missionaries, and they handed them over on July 23. The mob "rushed upon them from all quarters, pushed and dragged them till . . . they were stabbed to death, and their dead bodies dragged up and flung into the chapel."[9]

Edith Sherwood and Etta Manchester had gone to receive their eternal reward, having given their all to God and to China.

Raised in a wealthy English family, George Ward found Christ in 1890 during a meeting at the London YMCA. From the start the fruit of his salvation expressed itself in good works, and before long he was burdened by the needs of the

*George and Etta Ward*

mission field. Ward applied to the CIM, offering to meet all of his own expenses if the board accepted him. He accompanied the Thompsons to China in 1893, and after a time of language study he settled at Changshan in western Zhejiang.

Etta Fuller hailed from the American state of Iowa. She was orphaned at an early age when her parents passed away, but she found Christ at the age of 12 and later attended the Minneapolis Training Institute, departing for Zhejiang Province as a missionary in 1894. For the first three years she worked at Changshan, where her inner charm and beauty attracted the interest of George Ward. After their marriage in 1897 the Wards experienced a surge in their work, and in two years the number of Christians in Changshan doubled. In 1899 the arrival of a baby boy, Herbert, added to their joy.

On July 20, 1900, a friendly local magistrate advised George Ward to flee, for he could no longer guarantee the family's protection. Ward thought he should remain at his post, but made arrangements for his wife, five-month-old son Herbert and single missionary Emma Thirgood to leave for the coast the next morning. Ward didn't believe there was any serious danger, and promised his wife that if an attack on the city was launched he would leave immediately.

Etta Ward, her little son Herbert and Emma Thirgood left Changshan by boat on the afternoon of July 21. By evening they had only managed to travel about 10 miles (16 km) from Changshan when they looked back and saw a red glow in the sky above the town. They assumed the Boxers had arrived and were burning the city so they proceeded toward Quzhou, arriving at dawn the following day. The city was in an uproar due to the massacre of the Thompson family and other missionaries, and the boatmen refused to take the two women and child any further. Taking the missionaries' baggage, they threw it onto the riverbank, and ordered them to get off the vessel.

The besieged trio waited at the water's edge for a long time, until a boatman offered to take them to Hangzhou. They were relieved, but as they placed their luggage on the boat the same mob that had viciously killed the Thompsons arrived at the riverbank. Some of the men demanded money, at which Etta Ward took off her wedding ring and offered it to her persecutors. The leader snatched it from her and sneered, "We want your life, not your gold rings." Etta was suddenly:

> stabbed in the arm, and with a push she fell on her side. The crowd then seemed to fade from her sight, and all she saw was her babe needing to be fed from her breast, and drawing the helpless infant to her she pressed it to her bosom. The fiends then stabbed mother and child together, and with the next blow severed the mother's head from her shoulders, and so ended their sufferings together.[10]

George Ward, meanwhile, had escaped on foot with a Chinese evangelist and a servant named Li Yun. Traveling along small trails in an effort to escape detection, the trio were untroubled until the following afternoon, when they stopped at a village about 5 miles (8 km) from the city. When a hostile crowd surrounded them, Ward pushed past the mob and ran along a path, only to find that it came to a dead end at a pond. His assailants laughed at him as he returned; then:

> they set upon and beat Ward and his servant to death with sticks and clubs, and left the evangelist on the ground, also supposing him to be dead. He was not, however, even insensible, but saw all that was going on, and in the night crawled to a place of safety, and afterwards recovered.[11]

Emma Thirgood was a much loved English lady who from the time she was a young girl displayed a keen interest in spiritual things. Later, as a Sunday school teacher, she spent much time making sure each child under her care knew what it meant to

*Emma Thirgood*

be a born-again Christian. After gaining a passion for missions, Thirgood sailed to China in 1889. A short time later she told her family: "I feel I must write you a few lines to tell you how happy I am, and what great things the Lord has done for me. Is it not wonderful how he teaches us in China?"[12]

The initial excitement of life on the mission field wore off, however, and the constant exertions and stress of being a foreign woman in a strange land began to take a toll on Thirgood's health. By 1896, after seven years in China, she suffered a physical and emotional breakdown and returned to England, where she was described as "at the point of death."[13] After resting for two and a half years, Thirgood was given a clean bill of health and returned to Zhejiang refreshed and ready for the challenge. On the final Saturday before departing England she said, "My heart is full of praise to the Lord for having, after two-and-a-half years of waiting, so strengthened me that, contrary to the expectations of my friends, I am now able to return to the work I love."[14]

Emma watched in horror as the ruthless mob stabbed Etta and Herbert Ward to death. Seeing all this, "she knew there was no escape for her, and, kneeling in prayer, committed her soul to God. While in this attitude she received her death wounds, and thus obtained release from her cruel tormentors."[15]

The horrific slaughter of so many missionaries associated with the CIM was a devastating blow. Hudson Taylor had personally recruited and sent many of the workers to China. His health had been poor for some years, but the Boxer atrocities caused him deep grief, and he received his own call to heaven in 1905.

## Anti-foot-binding societies

Although the churches in Zhejiang were understandably shocked by the Boxer atrocities in the summer of 1900, the gospel rebounded surprisingly quickly, and by the following year reports were received telling of new growth and interest

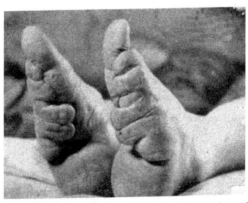

*A woman's disfigured feet after years of being bound*

in Christianity. One of the many effective ways the Christians used to reach people was through anti-foot-binding societies.

For centuries, Han culture had dictated that women must have petite feet, as it was considered a disgrace to have normal-size feet. Bound feet were seen as a symbol of beauty, especially among wealthy families where women's feet were bound in order to display their high social status, signifying that they didn't need to use their feet to work.

Young girls routinely had their feet forcibly bound and bandaged to stop their growth. The result was often a lifetime of misery for the women, as their deformed feet caused them to shuffle about in tiny steps.

Girls' schools established by the missionaries were the first to abolish the foot-binding practice among students, and non-Christian schools gradually followed their example. At Wenzhou, the local Biblewoman led an anti-foot-binding campaign. As she preached the gospel, encouraging women to both unbind their feet and surrender their hearts to Christ, the churches grew substantially. In many places the unbinding of feet was taught as an act of repentance, and new believers were instructed to show their allegiance to Christ by forsaking the wicked custom.

A Christian woman from a wealthy family was brought to tears because, although she had been tormented by her bound feet all her life, she had nevertheless also basked in the social standing the practice allowed her to enjoy. At a meeting, the woman reportedly prayed out loud:

> confessing with tears and sobs that her two feet were a disgrace to the Church. She finally said, "Lord, make me willing to unbind them, and forgive my sin in this." It was very touching, and there were not many dry eyes when she finished. Finally, nearly all who had not already unbound their feet did so . . . We have, altogether, over 120 signatures of Christian women

and inquirers who have unbound their feet since believing the gospel, and there are quite a few who have unbound without signing. This signature also pledges them not to bind their daughters' or daughters'-in-law feet.[16]

Foot-binding was ultimately outlawed in China, although old women with bound feet can still occasionally be seen hobbling along the streets of China's cities today.

## Wang Laijun—a pillar of the Zhejiang Church

Apart from the many foreign missionaries who gave their lives to serve the people of Zhejiang, God raised up a large number of key Chinese church leaders in the province. One of the most prominent leaders was Wang Laijun, who died in 1901 at the age of 72.

Wang, who led an extraordinary life for God, was born in a small village south of Ningbo in 1829. His reputation as

*Wang Laijun was a key church leader in Zhejiang for 46 years*

a skilled painter and decorator reached the ears of Hudson Taylor, who was residing in the city. Taylor hired Wang to do some work on his home, and it was there that he first heard the gospel. He surrendered his life to Christ in 1855, at the age of 26, and was baptized by Taylor.

When the great mission statesman returned to Britain in 1859, Wang accompanied him on the long journey. For the next few years he assisted Taylor in translating the New Testament into the Ningbo dialect, and he also helped new missionary recruits gain a basic knowledge of Chinese before they left for the Orient.

Wang proved highly capable, and at Taylor's suggestion the Zhejiang native studied medicine at the London Hospital, where he won the respect of the surgeons. Taylor had plans to establish a medical work in Ningbo, and Wang helped the vision become reality.

Finally, after five years in England, Wang Laijun returned to China where he preached the gospel and healed the sick. When the first church was established at Hangzhou in 1867, Wang was ordained as its pastor. He worked tirelessly at strengthening the faith of God's children in the city, and also established several outstations in the surrounding districts.

The same year he was appointed to lead the Hangzhou church, Wang's wife gave birth to their only child, a daughter. She later married a godly man, Ren Chengyuan. For decades Ren was a key leader of the body of Christ in Zhejiang, assisting his father-in-law in Hangzhou.

One Sunday morning in 1901, just after Wang had administered Communion to his church members, he was suddenly taken ill with fever. As he lay in bed, a malignant boil developed on his spine. Knowing his days on the earth were coming to an end, he summoned his loved ones and told them he was going to be with Jesus, and he appointed his son-in-law to handle his affairs and to lead the church. Wang then passed into the glorious presence of his Lord and Savior.

Those who knew Wang Laijun were keen to speak of his qualities and godly character. One tribute said:

> In character, Pastor Wang was diligent in business, meek and unobtrusive, kind, gentle and good to all; his speech and demeanor unblameable; faithful to his Lord and Master; sincere and reverent in his devotion, apt and diligent in feeding and nourishing the Church; impartial in his attitude toward and treatment of others ... He was ever ready to forgive and easy to entreat; forgiving and forgetting any ill-treatment he received at the hands of those who, at one time, were envious and jealous of his position and influence. Thus the heathen and church members alike respected and loved him, and received stimulus from his virtuous and godly example.[17]

## *The Church soars again*

Whereas many commentators lamented the future of the missionary enterprise in China after the Boxer massacres of 1900, the Church soon found its way back on track, and the years immediately following 1900 saw strong growth throughout Zhejiang. What wicked human beings intended for evil, God had turned for good, and many people testified that the godly and calm reactions by Christians to the brutal treatment they received had impressed them deeply and helped them see the truth of the gospel.

The first decade of the twentieth century had commenced with the diabolical massacre of many Christians, but it drew to a close in much more encouraging circumstances, with revival breaking out in various locations throughout Zhejiang. Missionary Edward Hunt reported how the churches in Wenzhou grew in the post-Boxer period:

From January 1898, until December 1906, about 700 souls have entered the church by baptism, making now a membership of nearly 900 [in Wenzhou City]. About 500 of these are men, and the remainder women . . . In addition to these church members, I suppose that there are about 1,500 regular attendants at our services.[18]

In May 1909, a missionary at Yongkang in the central part of the province excitedly reported how the Holy Spirit had visited their small church with great power:

We have had a great blessing. We have never seen the like of it throughout all our experiences in China. What happened was beyond all our anticipations. When we were in the midst of it, it was difficult to realize if we were dreaming or if the whole thing was a reality . . .

The confessions of sin, the crying, sobbing, and the extreme agony of not a few began and continued for two days. And what confessions they made! We were struck with amazement. They confessed to murderous intention, adultery, opium-taking, stealing, deceiving, lying, pride, hatred, jealousy, covetousness, indolence, hypocrisy. What awful revelations; it was difficult to believe our ears, to hear preachers, elders, church leaders, and members making confession of sins we thought they had given up long ago . . . It was the first time the white light of God's presence had illuminated their hearts and enabled them to realize their sins, as they had never done before.[19]

Throughout Zhejiang the work of the CIM had continued to steadily grow. By 1903, the mission reported a total of 3,756 baptized believers meeting in 90 churches throughout the province. Since the commencement of its work in Zhejiang in 1857, the CIM had baptized 6,607 people into the faith.[20]

James Meadows had arrived in China in 1862. In 1903, when he had already served for more than 40 years in Zhejiang,

Meadows reminisced about the astonishing changes he had witnessed in the province during his long career:

> When I first arrived in Zhejiang, in 1862, there were not 4,000 Protestant Christians in all of China. Ningbo was the only place properly occupied by missionaries. Now, thank God, we have 26 stations, 111 out-stations, and 73 missionaries . . . and 254 native helpers.[21]

The Catholic churches, meanwhile, had also grown in Zhejiang, with the work being administered by the Lazarists from Ningbo City. By 1907 they reported 25,126 believers, meeting in 153 churches throughout the province.[22]

# 1910s and 1920s

## A changing of the guard

The 1910s was a decade of transition for Christians in Zhejiang. Church leadership in the province continued to shift away from being in the hands of foreign missionaries to native pastors and elders. While in some denominations and mission groups the transition proved painful, others, like the CIM, were able to adapt more easily because of the influence of their leaders.

*Opening day of a new church at Zhengxian in 1918*

Hudson Taylor, the founder of the CIM, had always recognized that the key for future expansion of the kingdom of God in China lay with local believers. He once wrote:

> I look upon foreign missionaries as the scaffolding around a rising building. The sooner it can be dispensed with, the better; or rather, the sooner it can be transferred to other places, to serve the same temporary use, the better.[1]

Many of the missionaries in Zhejiang had given decades of sterling service to the Lord and His people, but the outbreak of the First World War devastated the financial resources of all groups. Donations dried up as Christians in the home countries focused on survival, and many of God's servants on the other side of the world struggled to get by. Hundreds were forced to leave China and return home.

More transition took place with the passing of key pioneer missionaries. Many who had arrived in the 1860s and 1870s died or retired after several decades of sacrificial labor. One saint who graduated to the side of Jesus was William Rudland,

*William Rudland*

who was one of the famous Lammermuir Party (named after the vessel that carried this group to China with Hudson Taylor in 1866).

In 1870 Rudland settled at Taizhou in southern Zhejiang, which was to be his home for the next 41 years until his death from a malignant tumor in January 1912. During those many years, Rudland firmly believed that the Chinese Christians held the key to evangelizing their nation. He desired to serve and encourage them to complete the Great Commission, but was careful not to take the lead in any matter the Chinese believers should have initiated themselves.

Although other members of the Lammermuir Party became more famous in the annals of China missions, Rudland was a quiet, unassuming servant who faithfully plodded along for his Master. He helped translate the Bible into the Taizhou dialect, and by 1898, after almost three decades in Zhejiang, Rudland reported that "31 stations and out-stations have been opened in the district of Taizhou, and 1,808 converts baptized."[2]

Two years after Rudland's death, the veteran missionary James Meadows also went to his eternal reward after 52 years in China. Meadows arrived in Zhejiang Province in 1862, and

*James Meadows served in Zhejiang for more than half a century*

his close relationship with Hudson Taylor dated back to before the formation of the CIM.

For over half a century Meadows endured great hardship. On numerous occasions he was abused and pelted with rocks, and he survived violent riots and robberies. His first wife died soon after reaching China, and his second wife perished during an influenza epidemic in 1890.

Most of Meadows' years in Zhejiang were spent at Shaoxing, which at the time was a hub of idolatry. When he arrived in the city there were only 42 church members, but "40 years later he was able to look back and thank God that no fewer than 788 persons had confessed their faith in Christ by baptism at that one station alone."[3]

In his final letter, written a few days before his death in September 1914, the 79-year-old veteran missionary wrote:

> Have I not had a long and full experience of His mighty love? How tenderly He has led me through this China wilderness! He is coming soon to take me to Glory. Since the breakout of the Great European War I have been longing night and day that the Lord Himself would descend from heaven with a shout, with the voice of the archangel, and with the trump of God. I long to hear the trump of God, and it will not be long now I hope.[4]

A tribute from fellow missionary Duncan Main revealed the great honor in which Meadows was held by all who knew him:

> Few have shown so noble an example of faithful service as he did, in the 52 years' hardship, toil, sickness, and suffering and long separation from the dear homeland, which during all these years he only visited twice. His large heart, perfect knowledge of the Chinese, his courage, his common sense, and his absolute loyalty to the great cause and to his mission, bound him very close to those of us who knew him best. He was truly a great missionary and a man with a very affectionate and unselfish nature.[5]

*Students at a women's Bible school near Wenzhou in 1912*

## *Fresh impetus*

The 1920s began with fresh impetus for the churches of Zhejiang. Growth had been steady in the previous two decades, and although many millions of people throughout the province had yet to hear the gospel, the new decade saw renewed efforts to reach the lost for Christ. In 1922 a missionary based at Xingu reported:

> Upwards of 2,000 villages have been visited in our evangelistic efforts throughout the year, not to count the many homes in this city that have been left with a word for the Lord . . . Gospels and literature have been sold and distributed to the number of some thousands.[6]

Statistics of the number of Christians in Zhejiang at this time were sketchy at best, although a 1904 survey of Evangelicals in the province had shown a total of 12,367 Evangelical believers.[7]

No more surveys were conducted until 1922, when *The Christian Occupation of China* revealed that the Evangelical enterprise in Zhejiang had nearly quadrupled in size to 48,079 believers.[8]

## *Ren Chengyuan—the apostle of the Zhejiang Church*

Each generation of the Church in Zhejiang seems to have had one key leader who faithfully showed the way forward to the children of God. For several decades Ren Chengyuan (also known as Ren Ziqing) was a key pillar of the Church in the province, which earned him the nickname "the Apostle of the Zhejiang Church."

*Ren Chengyuan*

Ren was born in Jiangsu Province in 1852, amid a time of great upheaval caused by the Taiping Rebellion. God protected him during those calamities, and at the age of 17 he believed the gospel and was baptized.

In 1874, a few years after his conversion, Ren was called to Zhejiang Province. At Hangzhou he met the esteemed church leader Wang Laijun, who was a close friend of Hudson Taylor. Ren immediately forged a deep connection with Wang, and a spiritual baton appears to have been passed down from one to the other. Ren married Wang's only daughter, and the remainder of his life was spent ministering in Zhejiang.

Ren was described as a Christian Nehemiah—a man who was skilled at dealing with the business of the Church, while maintaining a sterling reputation as a consecrated man of God. At a time when other Chinese church leaders struggled in their relationships with foreign missionaries, Ren enjoyed strong and mutual respect with a host of missionaries from different denominations.

For decades Ren Chengyuan provided wise and godly service to the body of Christ, helping the Lord's people through the diabolical Boxer onslaught of 1900, and proving himself a faithful guardian of the Church until his death from pneumonia in February 1929, at the age of 77. After his death, many tributes flowed in from those who knew him best. W. H. Warren, the CIM superintendent in Zhejiang, summarized Ren's life with these words:

> Pastor Ren was a man of outstanding ability, and would have been a force to reckon with in any calling in life. He early chose to walk in the way of the Lord, and amid all the vicissitudes of life held firmly to his guiding principle. Having set his hand to the plough he never seemed to look back, but with steady perseverance moved forward as led by the Spirit of God . . .

There is an association of Chinese pastors at Hangzhou, whose members hold regular prayer meetings. Pastor Ren was a tower of strength in such an assembly. Time and time again, when difficulties of church government or discipline have engaged the attention of the brethren, perplexed their minds, and presented an apparently insoluble problem, this man has sat, saying very little, with an inscrutable countenance, hearing and weighing all that the others had to say, then finally giving the clue, indicating the direction for action, and so finding a way through the maze.[9]

Eternity will reveal the full impact made by godly church leaders like Ren Chengyuan during the formative years of Christianity in Zhejiang, when a solid foundation was put in place for the mighty harvest of souls that were reaped for the kingdom of God in later generations.

## Dora Yu Cidu

A humble female doctor named Yu Cidu was one of the instruments God used to bring revival to His children during the 1920s.[10] Known in the West as Dora Yu, she was born in Hangzhou in 1873 and was raised in a strong Christian home. She later said that she was unable to recall a time when she did not love Jesus.

At the age of 15, Yu left home and traveled north to study medicine in Jiangsu Province, where she remained for eight years. She was engaged at 19, but soon realized that God's call on her life made her union untenable. She called off the engagement and remained single for the rest of her life.

In 1895, after receiving news of the deaths of both of her parents, Yu plunged into a pit of depression as she wrestled with feelings of guilt at not having seen them in their final days. During this pivotal time in her life, she wrote: "I feel in my soul

*Dora Yu Cidu*

this horrible feeling that I am standing at the edge of hell and may be pushed in at any time." Day and night she cried out for God's mercy, but the feeling of guilt lingered, nearly causing her to suffer a breakdown. Finally, after rededicating her life anew to Jesus Christ, Yu recalled:

> God suddenly opened the heavens to me and I was filled with the love of God Himself. I cried out to the Lord, saying, "Oh Lord, is this your love? It's like nothing I've ever experienced!" . . . Although I didn't hear God tell me that He had already forgiven all of my sins, I still felt His love fill my heart in that way. Those old feelings of conviction and fear suddenly disappeared without a trace.[11]

After being one of the first women to graduate from the Suzhou Medical College in 1896, Yu Cidu became one of the first female Chinese cross-cultural missionaries when she traveled to Korea and worked with an American ministry. For five years she labored in Korea, but something was missing. She ultimately realized she had gone there in her own strength and not in obedience to the Spirit of God. In 1903 she returned to China and once again experienced close communion with the Lord. She later described her time in Korea as her "wandering in the wilderness."

After returning to China, Yu felt the Holy Spirit calling her to abandon work as a doctor and to walk by faith, focusing on full-time evangelism. She never again received support from missionaries, but God provided for her every need.

Female evangelists in China were rare in those days and it was not culturally acceptable for a woman to travel around making religious proclamations. Nevertheless Yu pressed on, and soon filled an important role nurturing female converts who had been neglected by the organized churches.

In 1910 Yu held a summer Bible conference at which the Spirit of God deeply touched those in attendance, transforming their lives. The conference grew in size and became an annual event, emerging as a popular date on the calendar for many Christians. The conferences continued until the late 1920s, by which time many hundreds of women had been trained and called to full-time gospel service.

Another feature of Yu Cidu's ministry in Zhejiang was her effective outreach to women of high social standing. Females from wealthy families of that era were rarely seen in public, and as a result they became a secluded class cut off from society and subsequently from the gospel. God helped Yu break into those closed circles, and many women in Ningbo and other cities found Jesus Christ.

The impact of Yu Cidu's ministry was felt deeply for many years. In 1920 she traveled to Fujian Province where she led Lin Heping, the mother of Ni Tuosheng (Watchman Nee), to faith in Christ. Nee, who was 17 at the time he received the Lord, studied the Bible with Yu and went on to establish the Little Flock, which ultimately bloomed into a movement comprising thousands of churches and hundreds of thousands of believers throughout China.

For many years Dora Yu Cidu had carried ailments in her body, and growing pain caused her to step back from ministry. In 1931 she was diagnosed with advanced cancer, and she soon went to her eternal home.

# *1930s*

*A large group of Christians attending Bible school at Wenling in 1931*

## *A mighty revival*

Although it was still more than 20 years before the Communists took full control of China and declared the People's Republic, Zhejiang was overrun by Communist forces in 1927, which severely tested Christians throughout the province. By God's providence, Zhejiang had experienced powerful revival in the late 1920s, and this carried over into the 1930s, preparing the Church for the dark era that was to follow.

The 1930s was a time of great difficulty for the people of Zhejiang, with hordes of bandits roaming the countryside, pillaging and murdering their hapless victims. In the midst of the commotion, however, the wind of God's Spirit blew on the people of Zhejiang, and the hardships caused thousands of disillusioned people to seek shelter in Jesus Christ. Decades later, a church historian wrote: "During the 1930s a mighty revival swept through this region, leaving a large, dynamic church by the time of the Communist takeover in 1949."[1]

One catalyst for the revival in Zhejiang was the emergence of "evangelistic bands." Chinese preaching teams had been formed by evangelists in other parts of the country, and the concept spread to Zhejiang in the early 1930s.

As the revival spread throughout the towns and villages, the transformative power of Christ touched people from every walk of life. Rich and poor, young and old, were swept into the kingdom of God. At Taizhou, one man described as a "part-time fisherman, part-time bandit" listened intently to a preacher and his heart was deeply touched. The next morning he heard that a team of evangelists was going into the surrounding villages, so

*The ex-bandit preaching the gospel on the streets of Taizhou*

he tagged along to learn more about this new faith. The more he heard of the message, the more convicted he became of his sins. It was remarked that:

> He was thoroughly miserable, and yet unable to leave the men . . . He believed that Christ was the Savior and the joy of the Lord filled his soul. Day after day he went about with that evangelistic band with a heart bubbling over with joy, and before long he too was able to tell of this wonderful new Savior he had found.
>
> Naturally, a man like that was well known and his story was listened to by many who had been his former companions in sin. But no more was he to walk with them. His old life was over, and during the times when he was at home between his fishing trips, he went out all over the countryside with a bag of tracts on his shoulder and some gospel posters, seeking to catch men.[2]

*A street chapel at Wenzhou in the 1930s,*
*where inquirers were taught the gospel*

## Yongkang becomes a hub of blessing

The revival reached the central Zhejiang town of Yongkang in 1936. Although in most ways it was a nondescript town, the people of Yongkang had long been interested in the gospel. The first baptisms took place there in 1886, causing a missionary to write: "The people of Yongkang, the scholars, and even the boys, are most respectful and some are interested. A congregation of 40 to 60 regularly attend every Lord's Day."[3]

Later, a missionary couple, the Gracies, were assigned to Yongkang. In their 1906 annual report they stated: "1,542 services or meetings were held, 992 of these being in the city. The membership increased to 104, representing 42 towns and villages, while attendances in the city services increased to an average of 160."[4]

The Church in Yongkang continued to grow until the mid-1920s, when it fell into a slump due to the political upheaval and spirit of lawlessness gripping the country, and the number

*In 1937 Mrs. Lu was the oldest Christian in Yongkang, having been baptized 44 years earlier*

of Christians in Yongkang fell to half of their previous number. The revival of the 1930s therefore came at just the right time, and the Holy Spirit arrested the decline and again caused the light to shine throughout the blessed district. By the end of 1936 Yongkang boasted 518 believers in 16 congregations.

## A medium turns to Jesus

A startling conversion occurred at Yongkang when an old white-haired woman surrendered to Jesus Christ. She was widely known as a powerful medium who had often gone into demonic trances to communicate with the spirit world. One day she heard the gospel while listening to a Spirit-filled preacher, and a short time later a voice told her:

> "If you have anything to do with this Jesus I cannot use you. I have no use for you. He is true. Go to Him" . . . She turned from Satan to God and was gloriously saved by His grace. The woman met with much opposition from her husband and relatives, but the Lord protected her . . .
>
> All traces of idol and demon worship were swept clean from her home and found a place in the flames. The woman, her sons and her daughter-in-law were all baptized and now services are held every Sunday in her home where before it was a "synagogue of Satan."[5]

The medium's conversion was just one reason the revival blazed so strongly in Yongkang. In 1936 missionary G. W. Bailey visited the district and reported:

> The Church there still seems to be in the midst of a genuine revival, and we cannot but stand awed and praiseful as we witness what God by His Spirit is doing in their midst . . .
>
> We were overwhelmed when the leaders told us that there would probably be over 100 people ready for baptism at this time, and there were 126 men and women baptized during

those days. The examination of candidates took two days, and the men and women crowded the door waiting for their names to be called. What a motley crowd—youths and maidens, old men and women, blind, deaf, lame, all seeking baptism. Some were so old and feeble that we could not but feel they were only just in time.[6]

Yongkang has continued to be a beacon of spiritual light in central Zhejiang, and as recently as 2002 the Three-Self Patriotic churches alone reported 21,300 members in the city, meeting in 71 congregations.[7] Today, including unregistered house church believers, Yongkang contains approximately 80,000 Evangelical Christians,[8] and the city continues to shine as an example of God's forgiveness and love for the lost.

## *John Sung in Zhejiang*

Acknowledged as the greatest Chinese evangelist of his generation, John Sung (Chinese name: Song Shangjie) visited Zhejiang several times during his powerful but short ministry,

*John Sung*

leaving behind a trail of churches and redeemed people who met Jesus Christ and had their sins washed away.

During his visits to Zhejiang, Sung suffered terribly from the illness that would ultimately take his life in 1944 at the age of just 42, but he preached the gospel of repentance with great passion and power, spurning strong criticism from some denominational leaders and missionaries.

A marvelous breakthrough occurred in 1934 at Huzhou, where a man named Chung was the wealthy owner of a textile factory that employed more than 200 workers. He was renowned for his violent temper and debauchery, and was married to three different women.

One day Chung fell sick, and was admitted to the Good News Hospital. John Sung visited the patients that day, but Chung loudly abused the evangelist when he tried to lead him to Christ. A short time later, Chung's daughter was declared insane, but was delivered of demonic oppression after local Christians fervently prayed for her. This miracle deeply affected Chung, and Sung's personal diary recorded what happened to the transformed businessman:

> Chung realized that the gospel was true, so he confessed and repented of his sins. In Huzhu, 54 evangelistic teams were set up and Chung was selected their leader. I advised him to stop work on Sundays at his factory and give a tenth of his income to the Lord. These evangelistic teams witnessed to 20,000–30,000 people. I told them that the more they witnessed, the more filled with the Holy Spirit they would become.[9]

In December 1934, Sung visited the city of Jiaxing, where he stayed with the principal of the local high school. The man had been sharply criticized by many in the community for suspending the afternoon classes so that his students could attend the revival meetings. The Holy Spirit moved on the students' hearts, and before long a deep fear of God seized them. Thirteen ink pens were collected from students who had stolen them, while one boy who had received a cash prize for coming top in his class was convicted of the sin of cheating and apologized to the principal.

The meetings were open to the public, and one distraught man came forward and confessed: "My sin is too great. I set fire to the living quarters of someone I hated, and 72 people died."[10] John Sung assured the man that if he genuinely repented of his sins and surrendered his life to Jesus Christ, God would forgive him. He wasted no time in doing so.

The students had heard about the many miracles that accompanied Sung's ministry in other parts of China, and they desired to see God's power firsthand. Sung hadn't planned to hold a healing service in Jiaxing, but the evangelist's diary recorded:

> Miracles happened anyway. One 37-year-old beggar had 10 stiff fingers that couldn't bend. After he confessed his sins and prayed, the Lord healed him so he didn't have to beg anymore. A soldier who had been lame in the leg for four months could walk after being prayed for . . .
>
> I went to Jiangyin to hold meetings. The girl students from a Junior High School were especially responsive, with 204 of them repenting. In the message I called on the youth to dedicate themselves to God's service.[11]

John Sung's preaching style was often fierce and abrasive, and he didn't hesitate to rebuke other ministers of the gospel when necessary. At times, however, the Lord showed His servant that he had gone too far, and Sung was capable of applying balm to those whose conscience had been wounded by the sword of the Spirit. When Sung visited Hangzhou in May 1937, he noted:

> This time I did not upbraid the church leaders, but instead I exhorted and advised with love. Sure enough, Westerners and

Little Flock members gladly met together in one place. 691 people received salvation, and 222 patients were prayed for. The deaf heard, the blind saw, hemorrhages were stopped, and the violently demented were pacified.[12]

In 1938 John Sung returned to Zhejiang, but just after he crossed the Song River, the railway bridge was blown up by Japanese soldiers and there was no way to proceed by train. He finally reached Hangzhou by other means after much effort, covered in coal dust and badly sunburned. Despite air-raid sirens wailing all night, he was so exhausted that he slept soundly.

On August 25 Sung arrived in Wenzhou, and as soon as the local church leaders knew he had made it, the first meeting was arranged for that afternoon. About 2,000 traumatized people attended, and many were saved and healed of their diseases. Sung then moved on to the city of Wenling in Taizhou Prefecture, where he wrote:

Originally 3,000–4,000 had planned to attend, and room and board had been prepared for 600 delegates from various areas, but because of the dangerous circumstances and the threat of bombings only 100–200 came to the first meeting. Only a tenth of them could read the Bible . . .

After my urgent pleas to the Lord for help, the attendance increased daily, and I was able to help 572 persons to confess their sins and pray for salvation and the true spiritual gifts.[13]

## *The horrors of 1938*

After years of war and lawlessness had decimated Zhejiang, 1938 proved to be the height of misery as the Japanese army marched through the province, looting, raping and killing as they went. Previously admired as one of the most beautiful cities in the world, Hangzhou was reportedly reduced to being:

*Christian relief workers helping terrorized war refugees*

broken down and perplexed. The inhabitants have been smitten and made desolate, and their means of livelihood destroyed . . . Day after day, mechanized battalions poured into the city, and the heavy tread of infantry, and the clang of steel, made war a stark reality.

With the advent of this military machine, the residue of the populace was engulfed in terrible suffering and grinding oppression. It was pitiable to behold men, women and children cowed into a state of impotent terror. From the very first day this charming lakeside metropolis became a rendezvous of death and destruction. Hounded by fear and tortured with anxiety, trembling women and children ran hither and thither to hide from the assaulting hand.[14]

In the midst of this diabolical trail of destruction, all remaining foreign missionaries and many Chinese Christians poured out their lives to help the terrified population. Certain areas of Hangzhou, including the Red Cross headquarters and various mission compounds, were declared "safe zones." Within hours an estimated 25,000 women and children scurried to those places, hoping to gain refuge from the terrible Japanese, who had burnt down or demolished most of the homes in the city.

The American Baptist Mission was one of the Christian entities to open its land and buildings to the desperate. One missionary remarked:

> What a wonderful opportunity this presented to deal bread to the hungry; to relieve the fatherless and bring in the poor that have been cast out; to clothe the naked and plead for the widow; to visit the sick and bring healing balm to the wounded! . . . The other day, I came across a group whose faces were transfigured with radiant delight, for they had been born again, and bore the mark of belonging to the household of God.[15]

In the midst of the Japanese invasion, God preserved His children and many testimonies emerged of the supernatural protection of the Holy Spirit. When the air-raid sirens sounded, one young Christian man hurried into a bomb shelter, where he waited with 13 other people in a cramped space. When the Japanese planes had passed overhead:

> thinking the coast was clear he came out and encountered a Japanese soldier, who at once made ready to shoot him. He cried, "Wait a minute while I pray." Kneeling down, he prayed to the Lord to receive his spirit. When he opened his eyes, the officer asked if there were any more like him there, with the result that the whole lot were told to get away as quickly as possible.
>
> Another woman was praying in a Gospel Hall, which had only two days before housed over 100 refugees. She was the only

one left and was kneeling on the floor praying, when the place was badly bombed; the cross-beam of the roof fell in the shape of an inverted "V" above her head. Had she been standing she would certainly have been killed.[16]

The total number of Evangelical Christians in Zhejiang had been 27,902 according to a 1922 survey, and although no systematic research was able to be conducted during the 1930s, it is likely the number of believers in the province had increased to more than 100,000 by the end of 1939.

During the 1930s the most significant new church movement to emerge in Zhejiang was the Little Flock, which had been founded by Watchman Nee (Chinese name: Ni Tuosheng) in the 1920s. From the group's base in Shanghai, Nee trained leaders to spread the movement, and during the 1930s "the major expansion took place in the coastal provinces of Fujian and Zhejiang . . . By 1940, in Zhejiang alone, they had 262 assemblies with a total membership of 39,000."[17]

# 1940s and 1950s

*Missionary Frank England preaching on the street in Zhejiang in the 1940s*

## Prepared for burial

The new decade saw Christians in Zhejiang experience a continuation of the same kind of trials they had faced throughout the 1930s, with political and social upheavals failing to prevent the advance of the kingdom of God. Throughout Zhejiang, many spiritually hungry people pressed forward to taste of the Bread of Life.

One of the characteristics of the Church at the time was how people from all walks of life became disciples of the Lord Jesus Christ. At one baptismal meeting in Fenghua near Ningbo, missionary Maybeth Gray marveled at the myriad of different people who passed from death to life. She reported how God was:

> reaching every class and type with His wondrous salvation. There was a young farmer who had been attending services here for a long time now; there was a bright earnest young nurse from the city hospital, who loved the Lord and wanted to confess Him openly . . . There was a city businessman, who when he was examined for baptism said, "I've studied all China's religions and found they didn't satisfy—and then I heard the gospel and read the Bible. These religions were as small lamps that flicker and go out—but now I've found the Sun!"
>
> Last, but by no means the least, was an old lady of 84-years, who all her life had stored up merit in the eyes of the heathen by being a vegetarian. She heard the gospel, believed, and immediately broke her vow by eating fish. She came here for examination for baptism one Sunday afternoon. You could see she was nervous over such an ordeal, and she sat trembling on the edge of the chair.
>
> Finally she could stand it no longer; she got up, went to my desk and, laying her arm there and her head on her arm, she called out to the Lord in prayer: "Oh Lord, I am such an ignorant old soul, and I don't know anything. I don't know how to answer the questions they are going to ask me, but, Lord Jesus, You died for me, and I know You love me; now help me to answer right." She was called in then, but soon came out again . . . "The Lord helped me!" she smiled.[1]

As the 1940s continued, there was a growing awareness that the Communists would soon conquer the whole country and usher in a new form of government. Some Christians were unconcerned, believing things could scarcely be any worse than the decades of chaos under Nationalist rule. Other church leaders, however, saw how Mao's forces had acted in other parts of the country, and they did all they could to strengthen the flocks under their care for the anticipated onslaught.

The good news of salvation in Jesus alone continued to be proclaimed throughout the villages and towns of Zhejiang. By this time almost all Chinese evangelists were either living by faith or being supported by local churches. Few relied on foreign funding. This principle of self-support, which had been drilled into the Zhejiang Church perhaps more deeply than in any other part of China, was to greatly help the body of Christ survive the approaching storms of persecution. Whereas in other provinces many believers soon fell away when foreign funding was removed, in Zhejiang the Church continued to function in much the same way as it had been accustomed to for decades.

At Quzhou, a church member named Yi owned an inn and used the premises to witness for Christ at every opportunity.

*Two faithful Zhejiang evangelists in the 1940s*

Many guests were converted, and hundreds more heard the gospel for the first time and eagerly took literature back to their home regions.

One day a Daoist priest stayed at the inn. Yi explained the gospel to him, and the man confided that even though he had been a priest for many years, he didn't have any real faith in the idols. The next morning he asked Yi for a supply of gospel tracts, and then:

> Wearing all his priestly garments but armed with Christian tracts, he went to the busy railway station for the morning to give out tracts! The folk at the station were puzzled to know the meaning of it all. The priest told them that he had been a priest for years and knew there was nothing in it—idolatry was all a farce and utterly false, but that the tracts spoke of God and His Son who are real and living, and they alone can forgive sins and save people's souls. It made quite a stir.[2]

On October 1, 1949, Mao Zedong ascended a podium in Beijing's Tiananmen Square and announced the founding of the People's Republic of China. A wide spectrum of expectations existed among church leaders in Zhejiang, ranging from great hope for the future to dire predictions of doom.

The Spirit of God had been quietly at work for years, strengthening His children in Zhejiang in a marvelous way, and the Christian community had grown mightily both in grace and in size. One source later estimated there were 200,000 Evangelical Christians in the province at the start of 1950,[3] which means the Church in Zhejiang probably doubled in size throughout the 1940s. Author and China expert Leslie Lyall commented:

> Solid Bible teaching by Chinese teachers not only ensured the survival of the churches in the years of persecution to come, but also laid the foundation for the spectacular numerical growth

of the churches in the coastal provinces from the late 1970s onwards . . . A Sovereign God was even then, in 1949, preparing to manifest His glory to the world through this remarkable Church.[4]

## *A trail of tears*

The first few years of Communist rule in China proved relatively calm, as the government meticulously gathered information on the churches and all other citizens they considered a threat.

Most foreign missionaries had been expelled from China by the end of 1951. By 1953 Mao had done enough research, and persecution was suddenly ramped up against Christians throughout the nation.

In Zhejiang, the storm of persecution struck most severely in Wenzhou. Pastors were initially invited to come under the government's control, then ordered to submit. Those who refused to comply were branded "enemies of the state" and were called to endure years of brutal torture and hardship. Wenzhou had been identified as the heart of Christianity in Zhejiang, with one account saying:

> In 1951, when the missionaries withdrew from China, there were four or five large and flourishing churches in Wenzhou and hundreds of country congregations with a total of over 5,000 believers in this one city and the surrounding areas. Many of the merchants were Christians and ten shops in one street declared themselves closed on Sundays. The Christian influence on the city's economy was considerable.[5]

## *Wenzhou, the "religion-free zone"*

Wenzhou came in for special attention from the Communists, who were enraged not only at the number of believers there, but also that many of the leading business people of the city were devoted disciples of Christ.

The authorities decided to show their strength by crushing Christianity in the city, and they labeled Wenzhou a "religion-free experimental zone." The aim was to completely purge the city and surrounding areas of religious belief, particularly Christianity. The government mocked Christians by requiring them to implement a "Three Offerings and One Withdrawal" policy. They were forced to hand over church buildings, give up Bibles and turn in all religious materials. In addition, they were required to withdraw from church life.

By the mid-1950s, 49 pastors from Wenzhou City had been arrested and sent to prison labor camps in Heilongjiang—China's coldest province which borders Siberia. Most of the pastors received sentences of 20 years or more. They were forced to work 16 hours per day, seven days a week, rendering back-breaking labor in coal mines.

Just one of the 49 pastors completed his sentence and came back alive to Zhejiang.[6] Forty-eight others died from torture or exhaustion.

More than 1,000 miles (1,620 km) from home and unable to see any loved ones or hear news about the fellowships God had called them to lead, the Wenzhou pastors were cruelly isolated, and few facts are known about their experiences. What is certain is that the Lord Jesus recorded each cry of pain, their hunger and their aching loneliness, and He has wiped every tear from their eyes.

Many years later, the son of one of the martyred Wenzhou pastors shared his family's struggles during that dark time:

> As the Communists imposed their regime on the Chinese people after 1949, the suffering of Christians began in a subtle but real way . . .

First, guards ransacked our home, carrying away Bibles and other religious books, together with valuable items. Then they took my grandmother into custody, and later humiliated her by parading her through the streets with her two hands tied together behind her . . . Her elderly husband, a leader of a local congregation, was left sick and bedridden at home . . . Not long after this he passed away. God spared him from public humiliation and abuse.

Because of our family connections, we grandchildren were abused, ridiculed and treated as sub-human. We dared not enter or leave school by the main entrance or play with the other students during recess, for fear of militant schoolmates. We had become outcasts of society.

My elder brother was arrested for involvement in evangelism. He was a true man of God and also a respected and learned member of society. He subsequently died as a martyr in a Communist prison cell, leaving behind four children aged from 10-years-old to a few months . . . They all grew up to be mature Christians.

The next blow fell when my sister, the mother of young children, was arrested and publicly abused. She, too, was paraded through the streets, attracting big crowds of spectators. Her young children felt pain and shame at seeing their mother led through the streets with her head shaven and a board with a cross on it hanging around her neck . . .

The children used to hide from other children so as to avoid their contempt. When they took food to their mother in prison, they did so stealthily to avoid being seen. Not surprisingly, the children became rather introvert.[7]

The merciless treatment meted out to this one Christian family in Wenzhou was repeated countless times throughout the province. The persecution was designed to permanently obliterate Christianity, but many believers stood firm and refused to compromise their faith, even when hundreds of church leaders and key Christians were imprisoned throughout Zhejiang. Those who were not immediately executed were sent away for multiple-year prison sentences, never to be seen again.

Other pastors, however, were spared by secret Christians working in the police stations who risked their lives by giving advance warning of raids. Many families abandoned their homes and went on the run, some relocating to far-flung parts of China.

Even during the darkest hour, the body of Christ in Wenzhou and throughout Zhejiang maintained fellowship. Organized church meetings were no longer an option, but small groups of four or five believers discreetly gathered together in homes, barns or outdoors for Bible study and prayer. Just one Wenzhou pastor survived the horror of the labor camps. When he was arrested and condemned to prison, he left behind his pregnant wife and several children. Instead of falling into despair, however, the pastor:

*The Church in Zhejiang was left without leaders in the 1950s but learned to trust in Christ alone*

was able to minister comfort to others in similar circumstances. In spite of hostile threats and against friendly advice, he continued to preach Christ, running the risk of being even more severely punished. The Christians in Wenzhou took good care of his family and, when he returned after more than 15 years in exile, he found his children grown into adulthood and the family in excellent condition.[8]

## *The Lord has done it*

After Mao Zedong closed the curtain on China for a generation, little news emerged about the state of Christianity in Zhejiang Province. A survey of Evangelical churches in Zhejiang found

*Faithful Chinese Christians continued to share the gospel throughout Zhejiang*

there were 200,000 members in 1950, just before the brutal persecution began.[9]

Remarkably, it appears the number of Christians in Zhejiang may not only have held firm, but even increased during the 1950s and beyond. Although thousands of church members did fall away from the faith due to persecution, it appears they were replaced by new converts who were compelled to believe the gospel because of the purity and selflessness of the godly Christians around them.

The disciples of Jesus Christ in Zhejiang no longer counted their lives on this earth as precious, but had become a people who daily died to themselves and lived for eternity. This proved to be an unconquerable equation, and explains how the Church in Zhejiang later emerged as the province with the highest percentage of Christians in China.

In recent decades, historians have tried to understand the factors behind the size and influence of the Church in Zhejiang. Many, however, use mere human explanations to try to make sense of the phenomenon. They often assume that social factors were the cause, but they fail to understand the intervention and influence of Almighty God, as He preserved, cleansed and empowered His children.

Truly:

> the LORD has done this,
> and it is marvelous in our eyes.
> The LORD has done it this very day;
> let us rejoice today and be glad.
> (Psalm 118:23–24)

# *1960s*

## *The curtain closes*

The 1960s saw a dramatic change for the body of Christ in Zhejiang, and throughout the country. Persecution had been severe throughout the 1950s, but the new decade brought draconian changes as the government attempted to completely destroy Christianity.

For the next quarter of a century the Church in Zhejiang went almost completely silent. Very little news made its way out of China, and a concerned Christian world was left only with occasional crumbs and anecdotal stories. Many observers believed there would be no Christians left in the province after the Communists had finished their dire work, and that if missionaries were ever permitted to enter China again, they would need to restart their work from scratch.

*Christians in Zhejiang were forced to meet outdoors*
RCMI

One scrap of news did emerge from Zhejiang in 1961, when a Christian successfully mailed a letter out of the country. It brought great encouragement to those who had labored and prayed for the body of Christ in the province. The writer shared:

> It is impossible to describe all that I have seen in a short letter. But God's work is still going on gloriously in the lives of many faithful Christians. We must give praise and thanks to God for His gracious care and protection. In the past the Church was built upon sand, and now it is being built on rock. God does not make mistakes. I have been thankful to find brethren steadfast in their faith. This was seen particularly in many young people.[1]

## A decade of madness

The diabolical Cultural Revolution, which commenced in 1966 and continued until the overthrow of the Gang of Four and Mao's death in 1976, witnessed probably the most intense persecution of Christians in China's history.

Years later, a prominent house church leader from another part of the country provided insights into the dark forces that overtook the Communists during the 1960s and 1970s, which resulted in him and thousands of other Christians spending years in prison for the gospel. He wrote:

> Communism does something very evil to a person. It takes away the personalization of individuals. In fact, any social institution that systematically removes belief in God does this . . . When we are in Christ Jesus, it is not possible for us to torture others, because true Christians are conscious of a reversal of roles. It is impossible for a Christian to look into the eyes of a victim being tortured and not empathize with that person, even to the point of flinching with each blow.

Atheism takes that shared commonality away. Communism in China during those days dehumanized society. In accordance with evolutionary theories, people were devalued to the level of animals. People were no longer people; they were expendable. They were not thought of as sons and daughters, mothers and fathers, and brothers and sisters but as a collective, machine-like workforce that needed to produce more than it consumed.[2]

When new anti-religious regulations were implemented in 1966, Christians had no choice but to immediately cease all public meetings. Church buildings had already been seized by the government and turned into gymnasiums, warehouses and other facilities. Believers broke into small groups of no more than ten people, and strategies were adopted to ensure security as far as possible. For example, if believers agreed to meet in a certain home, they worked out a plan for each person to arrive at intervals 15 minutes apart, so that neighbors would not be alerted that a gathering was in progress. At the conclusion of the service, the participants also departed individually at regular intervals.

During the house church meetings, loud singing and preaching was not encouraged, and many Christians who owned properties soundproofed the meeting rooms as much as possible by hanging egg crates on the walls to deflect the sound inwards. Cracks were covered up around doors and windows, and believers were always on alert if strangers tried to attend a meeting, knowing they might be undercover agents.

In rural locations, believers often set up watch along pathways and roads leading to a meeting place. If any vehicle or unwanted visitor approached, a signal system was initiated to help attendees rapidly but calmly disperse in predetermined directions. On many occasions the Red Guards arrived at a location to arrest the Christians, only to find the place empty and all Bibles, hymn books and other evidence of a religious gathering removed.

Pressure from the government ebbed and flowed during these years, as God's children learned to discern when things were at their tightest and when they were a little more relaxed. For much of 1966 the environment was so tight that even small home gatherings were suspended. One account of the Church in Zhejiang told how:

> Small meetings resumed in 1967, but this provoked intensified opposition and fierce persecution. Christians were humiliated, tortured, threatened and subjected to "struggle" sessions. Many died in prison, while others were either killed or crippled by savage beatings. The survivors, however, emerged as powerful disciple-makers, although sometimes the only kind of public witness possible occurred at well-attended Christian funerals where full advantage was taken to proclaim a living Savior and a living hope. Even so, the funeral organizers were often arrested.[3]

Another source recalled the great sacrifice that many Christians willingly made to allow meetings in their homes:

> Christian gatherings never ceased completely, even during the Cultural Revolution. When political pressure ran high, churches went underground. As soon as the pressures relaxed, gatherings immediately resumed.
>
> Once, the police arrested a group of Christians gathered for prayer in a Christian woman's home. They left the woman free to take care of her household. However, as soon as she could find a friend to take her place, she hastened to join the arrested group. Such behavior bewildered the authorities, but she explained, "We Christians who suffer for the Lord on earth will receive a crown in heaven. I don't want to miss that!"
>
> The group was, as usual, paraded through the streets, but they had peace and joy in their hearts as their actions testified to the power and glory of the gospel of Jesus Christ.[4]

One young man from a Christian family gained a job teaching at a school in a nearby city. He was a believer in Jesus and had experienced His love and grace, but teachers were strictly forbidden to share religion with others, either in class or privately. If caught, the teacher would immediately lose his job and face prosecution.

After arriving at his new job, however, the teacher realized many of the students also came from Christian families throughout Zhejiang Province, and they needed fellowship with one another and Bible teaching if their faith was to survive. They met discreetly, and the power and presence of God was so strong in their meetings that they soon grew in number. While the entire social fabric of China was being torn apart, the Holy Spirit preserved this remnant of young believers and nurtured them in the faith. One of the participants later wrote:

> Some schoolmates of Christian students were killed in battles with different units of the Red Guards. But in Wenzhou, no God-fearing young people participated in the Red Guards' activities. They found safety at home with their families. At this time conflicts occurred not only on the streets between strangers, but also between husband and wife, father and son, brothers and sisters. Christians enjoyed love and care, not only within their own families but also with other Christian families.[5]

## *Plucked from the fire*

The Chinese government, despite all its efforts, was unable to quench the thirst that people had for spiritual truth. Indeed, it became evident that the disastrous policies implemented by Mao had caused a great spiritual hunger to rise in the hearts of many people, which ultimately resulted in a mighty harvest for the kingdom of God.

In the midst of terrible oppression and fear, the Holy Spirit roamed freely, blowing life into receptive hearts. One man named Li managed to flee to Hong Kong, where he spoke of the long and difficult path to salvation that he had walked down during the Cultural Revolution. When the Red Guards were doing their worst, Li recalled:

> Many were slaughtered. Stinking corpses were found alongside the streets and flowing down the river. Since there was nowhere to run, we waited for death at home.
>
> On a dark and quiet night, I was awakened by a nightmare. [In the dream I had seen] my mother kneeling in front of her bed, whispering, "Heaven, have mercy!" . . . My mother had been severely beaten so that her body was covered with scars and she lost consciousness. Yet, she had refused to submit or beg for mercy before.[6]

Although he did not yet know the Lord, the young man paid attention to the dream and wondered what it meant for heaven to have mercy on someone. In 1967 a series of terrible incidents struck Li's life, which ultimately led to him finding Christ. He explained:

> The dormitory where I lived caught fire. My clothes and hair were on fire. My body suffered serious burns and later festered. The people who came to put out the fire intentionally ignored me, and passed by me several times. Instead, they tried to "rescue" the works of Mao and his picture. My life wasn't even worth that of a tiny, pitiful beast . . .
>
> My mother was living in the female dormitory, about 300 yards away. She was in bed, very sick, when suddenly a strong force made her get up from her bed. She rushed out and cried hysterically. Pushing and shoving the firemen and the people around, she threw herself into the fire and rescued me. She later said, "There was a force moving me, but I didn't know what or who it was." This was the mighty

power of God, working and manifesting itself through my mother.[7]

After several nights in the hospital, the doctors warned Li that his nervous system had been permanently damaged and he would remain handicapped for the rest of his life. Three months later, however, Li was home alone in bed when suddenly:

> Golden light flashed through our small and crude lodging . . . At that moment, I had a feeling that I might be able to move. I moved left and right, and gradually I could sit up with the help of my hands . . . I moved toward the edge of my bed, and let my left foot touch the floor. As I did so, I immediately felt a warm current, like electricity, running through my hands and feet . . . I stood up on the floor and stepped forward. I was able to move slowly, away from the wall. When my mother returned home and saw me walking, she was astonished and for a long time could not utter a word. With her eyes wide open she stared at me and said, "Heaven has been merciful!"[8]

Some years later, Li heard about the Bible and tried to locate a copy, but all he could find in the county library was an old Russian Marxist book criticizing Christianity. After escaping to Hong Kong, he met other Chinese Christians who had fled the mainland, and he grew in knowledge of the truth. At the end of a long and difficult journey, Li joyfully declared:

> In my lowly and ignorant state, I am absolutely unfit to be used by God. But His abundant grace and desire to save people caused me to be enlisted in His army. He gave me this opportunity to become His disciple. I thank God for His gifts, His selection, and His working through me.[9]

Another well-known Zhejiang church leader during this dark period was Hu Zhenqing, who was arrested and sent to prison in 1958. He was released in July 1969 after spending 11 years in a prison labor camp, and he immediately resumed preaching the gospel. Hu was rearrested in 1973 and sentenced to another seven years behind bars. When he was finally released in 1980 at the age of 62, Hu courageously carried on his ministry, traveling widely and establishing churches throughout Zhejiang and Anhui provinces until his death in 1995. He is remembered as a man of God who was faithful even unto death, and whose zeal for the kingdom of God never waned.

At one place in the late 1960s, a group of ten Christian men and women were rounded up during a prayer meeting and hauled before an impromptu court. They were found guilty of "counter-revolutionary activities" and arrested, bound and viciously beaten in the public square as a warning to the rest of the community. As they were beaten, the believers preached the gospel at the top of their voices, imploring people to repent and believe in Jesus Christ before it was too late and they suffered His wrath.

When they could not be silenced, the guards flew into a demonic rage and blood flowed freely. The treatment meted out to the ten Christians was so savage that all the people stood still and watched in horrified silence. One account described the dramatic scene:

> Even the fortune-tellers were moved by the Holy Spirit and burst out crying. Many people hearing the Word forgot to eat, work, or even return home.
>
> The brothers and sisters preached until they were exhausted, but the crowd would not let them leave. The authorities, however, came and dragged the Christians away one by one, binding them with ropes and beating them with electric batons, knocking them unconscious. When they revived they continued to pray, sing, and preach to the bystanders.
>
> When the believers were bound and beaten, many people saw to their amazement that they were smiling. Their spirit and appearance were so lively and gracious that many were led to

*House church believers holding an impromptu prayer meeting in a public park*

believe in Jesus by their example . . . For more than three days they were left without food or water, beaten with sticks until their faces were covered with blood, their hands made black by the ropes—but still praying, singing, and praising the Lord . . . In this area the flame of the gospel spread everywhere![10]

## *Of whom the world was not worthy*

Throughout Zhejiang, many stories emerged of God's miraculous intervention on behalf of Christians who took a stand for Him during the 1960s. One young female science teacher refused to teach Darwin's theory of evolution to her students. For weeks the school tried to persuade her to change her mind, but she would not relent and constantly told them, "We are not monkeys. We are men and women made in the image of God."

When they realized their persuasions would not change her, officers were called in, and the young lady was forced to say the same words, this time through smashed teeth and bloodied lips. She was demoted to the role of school janitor, and the authorities forbade her from attending house church meetings with her fellow believers.

In another town, a respected doctor refused to say, "Chairman Mao is greater than Jesus Christ." Red Guards beat him unconscious and left him lying in a pool of blood on the hospital floor. When the guards returned a few days later, his reply was the same: "My Christ is bigger than Chairman Mao. My Christ is the Lord of Lords and King of Kings. He has been given the Name above all names in heaven, on earth and under the earth."[11]

The elderly doctor was beaten for several days, but he still refused to renounce his Lord and Savior. Finally, the Communists had enough of his insolence and decided to end the situation once and for all. They stripped the disciple of Christ naked and made him stand on a narrow bench, barely 6 inches (15 cm) wide. They taunted him to continue balancing on the bench, and threatened to kill him if he fell down.

After quietly repeating the biblical story of three young Jewish men who were thrown into a fiery furnace,[12] the doctor finally raised his voice to address his tormentors:

"They were not burned because the Lord stood with them, and He is with me now."

The hours passed, and not a muscle in his body trembled. Five hours, ten hours—people began to take notice. "Where does this old man get his strength from?" they asked. His very presence was becoming not only a witness to Christ, but a source of conviction and embarrassment to the others who saw him standing, naked, on the bench.

Finally, the cadre could stand it no longer. Naked, and without a whimper, the man . . . had stood, balancing himself on a narrow bench, from seven in the evening until ten o'clock the next morning. After 15 hours of what the doctor called "peace and fellowship," he was pushed to the floor. The Red Guards promised him that there would be another day. It came a week later. Dragging him away from his patients, they hanged him.

The guards fought among themselves. They were frightened. Some wanted to cut him down before he died. After a scuffle, one cut the rope. He fell to the floor and preached his last message: "As I was hanging there, my heart was melting for you." He then died, as his predecessor, Stephen, had done before him.[13]

A Zhejiang Christian named Chen was both an accountant and a gifted evangelist. Even in the midst of the Cultural Revolution, he shared his faith with his co-workers and sought to lead them to Christ. Chen even shared the gospel with a leader of the notorious Red Guards, a man who was deeply feared for his vicious and inhuman acts.

Chen invited the man to a house church meeting so he could hear the gospel and meet other Christians. Understandably, many believers were hesitant, but Chen finally persuaded them to trust God, much as Barnabas had once encouraged the early Christians to accept Paul into their midst.[14] At first, the man carried a pistol with him to the meetings, but after he accepted the Lord:

> His life was completely changed. He turned in his gun and resigned from the Red Guard organization. Not surprisingly, this action infuriated his superiors, who staged a public meeting to "struggle" against both him and Chen. They demanded that they either renounce their faith publicly or be demoted to sanitary workers . . . Sanitary work was a filthy and disgusting occupation. It required getting up at midnight to collect human excrement from each house and then carry the heavy load to designated locations.[15]

Both men accepted the demotions, and they were mocked as they began their new careers. Chen's family was deeply concerned about his health as he had never worked in a job involving heavy labor, and he had recently undergone major surgery. The duo committed themselves to the Lord, however, and each day they returned home and enjoyed rich fellowship, strengthening one another in the faith. Chen continued his job as a sanitary worker for 12 years until his retirement, and during that time he never once fell ill.

While many overseas observers believed that Christianity had died in China, as Marxist theory dictated, the truth gradually emerged that Jesus Christ was alive and well, and was living in the hearts of multitudes of followers throughout Zhejiang. Even during the darkest hours of the Cultural Revolution:

> Stalwart believers in dank prison cells and desolate rural fields were refusing to bow the knee to "Caesar." Choosing obedience to God rather than life itself, they persevered under unimaginable trials . . . Slowly, stories began to trickle out of brave Christians who had stood their ground through those long, lonely years. More than that, we began to hear about large-scale turnings to Christianity in rural areas where Mao's movement had once been strongest.[16]

# 1970s

## Nuggets of gold

One key aspect of the persecution endured by Christians during the Cultural Revolution was the destruction of Bibles. There was soon a famine of God's Word in Zhejiang, although believers in other countries prayed and were willing to attempt audacious things to help their brothers and sisters behind the Bamboo Curtain. In a foreshadowing of the twenty-first century—when South Korean Christians attempted to reach their counterparts in North Korea by floating "Scripture

*A clandestine house church Bible study in the late 1970s*

balloons" across the border—concerned believers in Taiwan tried to float gospel tracts and Bibles across the Taiwan Strait to Zhejiang and other areas of east China during the 1970s.

The Bamboo Curtain that descended on the Chinese Church continued to obscure the view from the outside world throughout the 1970s, but morsels of information occasionally emerged from Zhejiang. Stories that offered a glimpse into what was happening to believers in the province gradually increased as restrictions were slowly relaxed.

Several overseas Chinese Christians visited their relatives in Zhejiang, which provided a rare glimpse into the state of the Church at this time. Most reports since the 1950s had been grim and heavy accounts of mass arrests, martyrdoms and long prison sentences for church leaders, so stories about the normal functions of church life were eagerly digested by Christians around the world, who for years had been fervently praying for God's family in Zhejiang. One visitor shared:

> During the prayer time we all remained seated with our heads bowed. Those wearing caps had to take them off. Anyone who wanted to pray stood up and prayed aloud. One after the other they prayed as led by the Holy Spirit, and they all said "Amen" together at the end of a prayer . . . Their prayers, mingled with praise and thanksgiving, were mostly concerned with confession, with themselves, their families and others, and with their daily lives . . .
>
> Every sentence came from their hearts, and their supplication was based on the sure knowledge that God hears their prayers. The way they prayed revealed their incomparable faith in God. They know that they have to trust Him in their lives, and that to trust in themselves makes failure certain.[1]

In 1974, while still in the midst of the Cultural Revolution, one Christian returned to a rural area of Zhejiang to attend her mother's funeral. She reported:

Brethren collected pieces of wood to make a coffin. They invited more than ten young men to form a band and more than 20 others formed a choir. They prayed and sang at her home before going to the cemetery.

More than 80 people joined the funeral procession. The choir sang the hymn, "To God be the Glory" while they walked toward the cemetery. When they passed by the village school, their singing made many students, teachers and peasants come out and watch. They wondered why they sang so joyfully when their relative had died.

In the service, people stood around the grave to pray and sing. One of the Christian laymen witnessed to the crowd. He preached louder and louder, seeming to sense God's presence and strength on him. He said, "Jesus Christ our Lord is with us. Although our flesh dies, we will be resurrected in Him. We live here as strangers and one day we will return to our Father. I am not sad for her death. I am happy and at peace for she has been received into heaven with Jesus Christ."[2]

When the preacher's voice increased in volume, some of the believers cautioned him that saying too much would land him in trouble. The zealous brother, who had already spent much time behind bars for his faith, replied, "We are believers, and we must witness for Him and not fear prison! God will take care of us."

## Supernatural power wins many to Christ

Prior to the expulsion of foreign missionaries in the early 1950s, the Church in Zhejiang had largely grown through solid Bible teaching and zealous preaching of the gospel. Few missionaries or Chinese leaders at the time taught or demonstrated the power of the Holy Spirit like the first Christians in the New Testament. Many Christians believed in cessationism—the doctrine that the era of spiritual gifts and miracles ended when the last apostle died. For more than a century the Evangelical churches of Zhejiang had mostly agreed with this belief, with occasional exceptions to the rule.

During the 1960s and 1970s, however, Christians in Zhejiang were stripped of all outside props and were separated from foreign influence. Instead, simple-hearted believers were forced to cry out on their knees to God, and He answered their prayers. God baptized them with the Holy Spirit and with fire, and supernatural miracles reappeared, not in a contrived manner, but as a genuine and transformative reality that met the needs of desperate people whose lives had been crushed by decades of oppressive rule.

In 1976 a Chinese believer managed to migrate to the United States from a village in rural Zhejiang, and described how an entire Communist production brigade had turned to Christ, despite the tense atmosphere. She shared the following insightful testimony:

> In that particular production brigade there were two or three families who were unusually zealous for the Lord. They were willing to pour themselves wholly into prayer for the salvation of the entire brigade. They helped everyone who needed their help, and the non-Christians in that village were exceedingly moved. They felt it was great to be a Christian, so they, too, believed in the Lord . . .
>
> Wherever Christians are active, the devil is also extremely active. At one time there were many in that village who were possessed by demons. Not a few were mentally ill, too. All the Christians prayed for them and they were healed, and the demons were expelled. There was real power in the prayers of the Christians. When they prayed for the demon-possessed, the demons fled, but if a person did not confess their sins thoroughly, the demons returned to them, and they became re-possessed. But if the whole family prayed sincerely and wholeheartedly, and the demon-possessed person confessed their sins thoroughly, the devil fled and never returned . . .

In a neighboring village the mother of the secretary of the Communist Party was a Christian. She was once very sick and sought help from doctors everywhere, but they could not help. As a final resort she asked friends to invite Christians to her home and pray for her. The believers prayed regularly for two months, and finally she was healed. She became an earnest believer, and the Christians began attending meetings at the cadre's home![3]

The result of these demonstrations of God's power was that multitudes of desperate people throughout Zhejiang were attracted to the gospel, and the Holy Spirit ensured that once again the plans of wicked human beings to destroy His work were doomed to fail.

The same Christian from Zhejiang shared how the house churches managed to arrange fellowship and how they were fed by God's Word during the Cultural Revolution:

Usually those who lived near each other got together. Someone would get the word around, and we would all gather together. Often there were no preachers available, so we didn't have anyone to teach us. Not many of us could preach, but many elders from the pre-Revolution days assumed the responsibility of preaching. Whenever an elder came to a village, word of his arrival would spread, and the Christians would come together for Bible reading, prayer, and fellowship.[4]

## God's wrath leads many to repentance

On a number of occasions in Zhejiang during the 1970s, peculiar incidents of God's wrath befell persecutors of the Church, leaving unbelievers in no doubt that the living God had punished those people for their evil acts.

In one village, a group of poor Christians were often prevented from gathering by a female officer, who seemed to hold a personal grudge against the body of Christ. One day, fed up at being harassed and deprived of fellowship, the brothers and sisters in that village prayed, asking God to turn the situation around and to stop the woman interfering. The Heavenly Father heard their prayers, and a short time later:

> The legs of the female officer became paralyzed and she couldn't walk, so she couldn't come to disturb them.
>
> The police chief at that place had a pig at home which suddenly died for no reason. Then within a week another pig died . . . Nobody dared reprove the chief for his actions against the Christians because he was such a ruthless man. But God used the mouth of his wife to do this. She said to him, "Look what you have done. What does people's worship have to do with you? You are ignoring your own affairs, and always interfering with others. Look at this. Two pigs have died. You really did it!" The chief couldn't say a thing in response, but from that time on he never bothered the believers again.[5]

Similar displays of God's wrath fell upon persecutors in other areas of Zhejiang during these crucial years when the Spirit of God was purifying His Church and preparing it to bring in a great harvest. One cadre who constantly cursed God suddenly developed an ulcer inside his mouth and died. In another bizarre incident, the tongue of a Public Security officer reportedly "hung out of his mouth down to his chest. He went to various hospitals in Hangzhou, but the doctors told him, 'This sickness is incurable. We have never seen such a problem before.' He couldn't eat or speak."[6]

Later, somebody told the man, "You have cursed God. You had better beg Mrs. Zhou to pray for you. If she doesn't pray for you, I'm afraid you will die." The man wasn't humble enough to visit Mrs. Zhou himself, but he asked his wife to visit her and ask for prayer.

After welcoming the officer's wife, Mrs. Zhou asked her, "Is your husband willing to repent of his sins and blasphemies? If he is ready to repent, tell him he must show his willingness by coming and seeing me himself."

The man's peculiar condition worsened, until he finally cast off his pride and visited the Christian woman's home. She preached the gospel and asked if he was willing to repent of his sins and believe in Jesus Christ. He nodded his head and she prayed for him. While she was still praying:

> His tongue slid back into his mouth. News of this incident spread far and wide. There was no need to preach the gospel there. All the people came and wanted to listen to the Word of the Lord. The Lord Himself came to save . . . They hurried to come, and were thirsty . . . They wanted to understand His saving grace and learn the Way of the Lord Jesus. All this was God's own work.[7]

## Back from the brink of death

In another part of Zhejiang, a woman with an incurable disease was perishing quickly. A doctor declared she was about to die and instructed her family to move her body to another room. Mustering her last ounce of energy, the woman sat up

*A rural house church meeting*

in bed and called out, "Jesus, save me!" Within hours she was completely healed. The doctor was shocked, and news of the miracle soon spread throughout the district, convincing many of the truth of the gospel.

In another village an old man lay in bed, having suffered from a serious leg infection for years. Blood and pus constantly oozed from the open sores, and even his own children wished he would die to ease his pain. He was scarcely able to sleep at night and continually scratched his sores in a bid to ease his discomfort.

News reached the village about the woman who had been healed by Jesus, and the sick man immediately begged his nephews to take him to her house. With tears in his eyes, the desperate man said:

> "Auntie, I heard that when you were about to die, a doctor named Jesus came to bring you back to life. Where is this doctor now? Please call him to heal this pitiful man!"
>
> The woman laughed and said, "Jesus is not a doctor who carries a medicine box, and I can't really tell you much about Him. I only know that when I called out His Name, I was healed!" . . . She then cried out, "Jesus, I ask you to come and have pity on this old man!"
>
> After crying out to the Son of God several times, the emissions from the old man's sores stopped flowing, and within two days he was healed![8]

News of these remarkable healings spread like wildfire throughout the rural communities of Zhejiang, but few people understood the gospel at that time. Many just thought the Name of Jesus had supernatural power and was a kind of magic potion for people's illnesses.

One day a believer's four-year-old son drowned while swimming in a river, and his body was recovered and placed on the floor in the middle of the house. The entire family knelt down around the body and prayed with great fervency, "Jesus, save this child! We have heard that you heal many sick people and we deeply believe you can bring this dead child back to life." As the family continued to cry out to the Lord:

> Suddenly a witch who lived nearby shrieked, "Your Jesus has come! Quickly, come and see!" The roomful of believers immediately opened their eyes and saw the child sitting up, but they did not see Jesus. Then the witch said to them, "When you shouted 'Jesus' loudly, a man appeared whose body shone brightly and whose face was full of love. He placed His hands on the child's head, and he got up. Your Jesus is truly amazing. He is the true and living God. From today I renounce my previous beliefs and I now believe in your Jesus."
>
> She then asked several brothers and sisters to go with her to destroy her idols, incense altar and all the artefacts used in her superstitious worship.[9]

## *Prayer causes an earthquake*

An extraordinary incident occurred at Lishan village after a baptismal service was interrupted by the Public Security Bureau in 1973. Dozens of new believers had gathered, eager to display their faith by obeying Jesus' command to be baptized. Because of the large gathering, participants were told to meet at several places around the village before proceeding to the river at midnight for the baptismal service.

The local authorities were alerted to the plan and paid 90 thugs to hide nearby. They collected wheelbarrows full of manure which they intended to use to mock the Christians by floating it downstream once the baptisms commenced. They also prepared a mound of stones to throw at the new converts as they emerged from the water.

The believers of Lishan discerned that something sinister was being plotted against them, so they immediately knelt down and prayed to their Heavenly Father. They cried out, "Lord, have you not been given all power in heaven and on earth? You blinded the eyes of those wicked people in Sodom. Lord, we ask you to use your unlimited power to perform a miracle and deliver us today."

As the brothers and sisters prayed, the Holy Spirit fell upon them. They felt they should not wait until midnight to start the service so they immediately began singing and praising God. Four to five hundred believers had gathered by this time, and they sang with such energy and excitement that the sound could be heard in neighboring villages.

The glory of the Lord descended on the Lishan believers that evening. They felt as if they had entered into the glorious presence of the Almighty, and they began to sing in unison: "Be faithful, be faithful, and proclaim this message everywhere; be faithful in that which has been committed to you; be faithful to your glorious King . . ." It seemed to the Christians that they were almost floating in God's presence as they sang this battle song over and over. Suddenly:

> the place began to shake and dust fell from the ceiling. Then the houses in the village all began to rattle and even the hills rumbled and shook.
>
> Several sisters were at home washing bowls when they felt the ground shake beneath them. Windows and doors shuddered and crockery rattled. Their hearts also shook! . . . The worship went on for another two hours. Then a brother was asked to speak, but he declined, saying, "I have believed in the Lord more than 50 years, but never have I seen a meeting like this. How can I stand up to speak?" . . . He led the crowd to a deep pool beside a stream where 78 brothers and sisters were baptized.
>
> When the 90 thugs hired by the authorities to break up this baptismal service heard the sound of singing that shook heaven

and earth reverberating throughout the whole village, shaking the very ground they were standing on, they took off in fright![10]

## *Prolific growth*

After Mao Zedong's death in 1976, China was once again plunged into a period of uncertainty, but the most brutal anti-Christian persecution appeared to decline, and believers throughout Zhejiang felt the first rays of sunshine on their faces after a long and bitter winter.

The year of 1978 seemed to mark a major turning point in the Zhejiang churches, as believers grew more confident that their meetings were less likely to be raided. The veteran British missionary Leslie Lyall, then aged in his seventies, wrote several excellent books in which he pieced together all the snippets of available information about what had happened to the body of Christ in China over the previous quarter of a century. Writing of the churches in Zhejiang Province, Lyall noted:

> In 1978, a powerful work of the Holy Spirit began bringing to Christ men and women by their thousands, including large numbers of young people. The growth was prolific, and renewed persecution failed to quench the fires of revival; even children remained true to their Lord despite threats from their teachers . . .
>
> After 1978, cottage meetings again began to multiply throughout the province, some starting in a small way but others, like the one in a village with 1,000 believers, growing in large dimensions. In one mountain region of 10,000 people, one in three of the population had become Christians, meeting in 15 church centers . . .
>
> One fellowship held retreats and training classes for young converts in the nearby mountains, and baptized 100 people in a mountain stream. Militiamen dispatched to prevent the

baptisms thought they saw soldiers surrounding the Christians and so withdrew their detachment in the belief that the army had the matter under control; but there were no soldiers, and the baptismal service proceeded without any interference!

In some rural areas over 90 percent of the population are Christians—a totally unprecedented statistic in the history of the Church in China . . . One semi-official estimate is that in Zhejiang alone there may be as many as five million Christians.[11]

While many marvelous evidences of God's grace and power were seen throughout Zhejiang in those special days, Satan was not far behind, sowing tares among the wheat in an attempt to spoil the harvest. In one county, a self-proclaimed prophet told people to gather together and wait for the Lord's return. He had previously instructed them to hand over their money and other possessions. One source sadly noted:

Because the brothers and sisters didn't have any Bibles and had never heard sermons on biblical truth, they thought this man was right and did what he said. Some of them sold their houses, some sold their furniture and clothes, and they handed the money to this crook. He also told them to make white robes which they were to wear on the day that the Lord Jesus would return. He told them to go up a mountain together and wait for the Lord.

The brothers and sisters obeyed him and bought white cloth to make the robes, and on the set day they went up the mountain together. They waited from the morning to the afternoon, and nothing happened . . . The crook told them to pray, and everyone knelt down to pray.

While they were praying, the crook ran away. Meanwhile, the cadre of the commune saw this strange group wearing white robes gathered on the mountain and wondered what they were doing. They surrounded the mountaintop and arrested the brothers and sisters.[12]

## *Prepared for a new dawn*

A new challenge faced the Zhejiang Church by the end of the 1970s. The government had increased the profile of the Three-Self Patriotic Movement (TSPM), and pressure was being placed on all unregistered house churches to join this state-approved organ. Those who chose to register were promised freedom of worship, but those who continued to ignore the edict potentially faced years of continued harsh persecution.

Some church leaders had already spent years in prison and flatly refused to have anything to do with registering their churches with an avowedly atheist government. Many believed that registering was akin to denying Christ.

Other Christian leaders in Zhejiang, however, saw the potential of a positive change and more freedom for the gospel to spread. Godly men and women on both sides of the argument were entrenched in their positions, but there was also a group in the middle who wisely advised the pastors and elders not to reach a hasty decision, but to wait upon the Lord and pray until the Holy Spirit gave clear direction to His Church.

The same challenge faced Christians in all parts of China, but the believers in Zhejiang—and Wenzhou in particular—came to a unique conclusion in the early 1980s. Their Spirit-led decision may have been the catalyst for the surge which has resulted in the province having the highest percentage of Christians in China today.

# 1980s

## The "registered house churches" of Wenzhou

First-time Christian visitors to China today often expect to find a persecuted, underground body of believers who meet in caves, apartment blocks and other nondescript locations. Those who visit the coastal Zhejiang city of Wenzhou would be shocked by the overt and dominant Christianity on display there, with thousands of churches—dozens capable of holding in excess of 1,000 worshippers—dominating the landscape,

*One of the hundreds of "registered house churches" in Wenzhou today*
Pieter Kwant

149

both in the city itself and in surrounding districts. Believers like to say there is "a church every kilometer" in Wenzhou.

Many overseas visitors have mistakenly assumed that the situation in Wenzhou is representative of all of China, when in fact the open churches there are a special arrangement not seen even in other parts of Zhejiang Province. How did this come about?

In the late 1970s and early 1980s the government-approved Three-Self Patriotic Movement grew in influence, and the authorities dictated that all Christian fellowships must register with them or face the consequences. The Wenzhou church leaders prayed fervently, seeking God's will, but pastors and their flocks seemed hopelessly divided. Some believed that to register with the government was akin to denying Christ, while on the other hand there were many genuine believers who feared that not registering as Three-Self churches would be disobeying the laws of the land and the civil authorities instituted by God. Many pastors did register with the TSPM, and hundreds of new church buildings sprang up throughout the region.

Wenzhou by this time had emerged as a powerhouse for Christianity, earning it the nickname "the Jerusalem of China." Many children of faithful Christians had risen to positions of authority in the local government, and were not inclined to rigidly enforce the harsh edicts against the Church that were handed down from Beijing.

Wenzhou's economy had also emerged as a major force in China, with the city rivaling the combined economic output of the much larger Beijing and Shanghai. The new leaders of China in the 1980s were eager to develop the country's infrastructure to catch up on decades of lost progress under Mao, and they needed to curry the favor of Wenzhou business leaders, many of whom were dedicated followers of Christ.

This unique environment resulted in the praying Wenzhou church leaders reaching a unique arrangement. Instead of deciding which side to take in the registration question, they chose neither to close their fellowships nor to register with the government. All across Wenzhou, large house church buildings emerged, independent of the Three-Self yet openly proclaiming the gospel. They came to be known as "registered house churches." With the possible exception of some tribal areas in southwest China, this arrangement is unique to Wenzhou.

It appears the Chinese government was certain that Christianity in Wenzhou would gradually fade into obscurity as the older generation of believers died. The atheist leaders of the nation saw no value in religion, and assumed the people of Wenzhou, being highly educated and economically prosperous, would abandon their faith. They were unable to comprehend that Christianity is not merely a set of man-made rules or human philosophies, but a personal relationship with a living Jesus Christ.

Communist hardliners who had arrogantly instituted the "religion-free zone" of Wenzhou in the 1960s were confounded by the wisdom of God. The Church in Wenzhou continued to flourish, and became a highly visible sign of both the triumph of God's kingdom and the foolishness of those who attempt to destroy it.

## Huang Detang's contract with God

On April 15, 1981, an elderly man of God named Huang Detang was lowered into a grave in Xiangshan County near Ningbo City. Huang had never been an ordained pastor, but had lived out his faith as an uneducated farmer. The surrounding communities had such respect for Huang that more than 400 people paid their final respects at his funeral, even though it had not been advertised.

Huang first believed the gospel when he was in his forties. Years later, he developed painful boils on his feet which caused him great agony and prevented him from working. Locals gave him the nickname "Lame Huang."

In his desperation, Huang cried out to Jesus for healing. A short time later he received a vivid dream, in which the Lord told him, "You must truly believe in Me, and I will heal you. You must witness for Me."

In his dream, Huang thanked Jesus for the help he would receive and promised that once he could walk again, he would share the gospel widely. Huang said the Lord told him, "A verbal promise is not enough. You must write a contract of indenture by which you offer yourself up as My servant."

Huang had only a primary school education and didn't know what a contract of indenture was or how to write one. He again cried out for God's mercy and help, and received another dream in which the Lord showed him how to word the contract. Huang composed the following:

I, Huang Detang, sign this indenture by which I offer myself up forever.

Because of my own uselessness, I have boils on my feet. They are very painful and I have nowhere to turn. I can only ask my gracious Savior, my Lord Jesus, to be merciful to me, a great sinner.

I now receive the precious Blood of the Lord as the ransom price which has redeemed me from death to life, and I know that the Lord will heal my feet, take my soul to the heavenly kingdom forever, and I will become a child of God with honor and glory.

Because I have nothing to repay the grace of God, I will most gladly dedicate my body and soul to Him. After my dedication,

I am totally at the disposal of the Lord. No matter where I am sent, even without any address, I will go. Whether it is to the east, south, west or north, whether it is climbing mountains or crossing seas, cold or hot, whether I am hungry or thirsty, or if I suffer want and persecution, I will follow the Lord to the end and not be disheartened. No one in my family or among relatives and friends will be able to pose any obstacles or cause me to go back on my promise.

This indenture is the common wish of both parties and neither of them raises any objection. I sign it as evidence of my willingness.

Huang Detang.[1]

A short time after he signed his unique contract with God, the boils on Huang's feet disappeared and he was able to walk freely again.

Over the years, each of the points in Huang's solemn contract was sorely tested, as God took Huang at his word and stretched his faith by sending him on dangerous adventures that resulted in thousands of people hearing the gospel. From the 1950s to the 1970s he ministered, during the darkest days of Communist persecution, and was arrested and tortured by the authorities on several occasions.

Huang's ministry was characterized by many instances of God prompting him to do things that made no rational sense, but with his indenture in mind, Huang obeyed the prompting of the Holy Spirit and remained true to his pledge, even when it resulted in great personal hardship. On one occasion when Huang was preaching he heard the inner voice of the Spirit of God tell him, "Love the one in the last row!"

That night he was unable to sleep, and at dawn he met with the pastor and inquired who the person was who sat on the last row of the church. Huang was taken to a tiny shack, where he saw a bedridden man with only a tattered blanket on his bed, and dirt covering every inch of the room. The man's limbs were pale, and only when Huang saw the man in the light did he realize he was a leper.

Brother Huang asked the man how many years he had believed in Jesus, but he just shook his head to indicate he was not a Christian. He asked the leper why he had gone to the church the previous night, and he replied that he had received a dream instructing him to go to the meeting because Jesus wanted to save him. On the day of the meeting he was able to get out of bed for the first time in months, and a neighbor helped him to the church.

Huang Detang didn't know how he could help the man's dire situation, as he was impoverished himself. Then the Lord told him, "Take off your jacket and give it to him." Huang was afraid. His padded jacket was the only one he owned. It kept him warm as he walked through the mountains in winter, and he slept in it while on his preaching journeys. "Surely not, Lord. I have great need of it," Huang argued. The Holy Spirit said to him:

> "If you do not give it to him, what you preach is like a noisy gong or a clanging cymbal. If you have not love, what use is it? If you have not love, you are not serving Me."
>
> Brother Huang had to obey in tears, but as soon as he had given his jacket away he felt immensely relieved . . . He was without a jacket for many years and yet was not frostbitten.[2]

Sometimes the demands God placed on Huang were too difficult for other Christians to cope with, and they refused to be involved. One of those times was when the Lord directed him to share the gospel and demonstrate God's love to a disheveled prostitute, who was near death from syphilis. Huang shared the gospel and provided her with food and clothing. The ladies in the local church, however, did not want to stoop so low as to help such a wretched person, but due to God's love shown through Huang, the woman died a short time later as a follower of Jesus.

Huang continued witnessing for his Lord and Savior right up to his death in 1981, at the age of 96. Few people outside his home region in Zhejiang have ever heard of Huang Detang, but in heaven he is known as the man who kept his contract with God.

## Persecution in central Zhejiang

New government religious policies were implemented throughout Zhejiang in the early 1980s. As a result, numerous new buildings were opened as places of worship, while many old churches that had been confiscated in the 1950s and 1960s were returned to the body of Christ. From the opening day, the churches were crowded with large numbers of spiritually thirsty people. Some were faithful believers who had

*Hundreds of believers jammed into the Wuniu Three-Self church in the late 1980s*

155

persevered during the Cultural Revolution and were delighted to be able once again to freely worship God. Other attendees were curious locals who wanted to see what Christianity was about.

Although many churches in Wenzhou were permitted to operate openly without registering with the TSPM, this unique arrangement didn't extend to other parts of Zhejiang, where the government severely persecuted house church believers who refused to join the Three-Self.

The majority of Evangelical churches throughout the province had declined to register, and their stand seemed justified when reports surfaced of the active participation of TSPM officials in the persecution of Christians.

Yiwu City at the time contained approximately 20,000 Christians, most of whom had agreed to register. A similar number of believers in nearby Dongyang, however, decided to remain independent, which enraged the local Three-Self leaders. They ordered more than 100 illegal house church fellowships in the county to disband and to attend Three-Self churches instead.

On February 28, 1982, Jin Bingfu, the deputy chairman of the Three-Self committee in Dongyang City, incited commune members and the militia to launch a sudden attack on a house church meeting during the Sunday morning service.

At first the attackers tried to intimidate the congregation, and when that failed they threw chalk dust into the air to blind the believers. They then used electric batons to torture the church members, and several women fainted after their bodies were jolted by the electric current. As they lay unconscious on the floor, their clothing was removed and they were left naked in a bid to humiliate them.

Finally, some of the believers were beaten and thrown into manure pits near the church. One brother, who refused to stop praying during the commotion, was bound, stripped naked and hung upside down. He was beaten until he was black and blue all over, but still he persisted in prayer. Months later, one of the men who had been battered and thrown into a pit died from his injuries.

Thirty-one believers at Dongyang were arrested and locked up at the Public Security jail. When news of the shameful attack spread throughout the local community, both Christians and non-Christians marched on the police station and demanded the believers be released. The officials finally bowed to public pressure and let them return home. No action was taken against the leader of the Dongyang Three-Self church who had instigated the attack.

The persecution at Dongyang did not end there, however, and a short time later the house church leaders were again arrested and tortured. Meanwhile, a sizeable number of Christians who had registered in neighboring Yiwu were disgusted when they heard about the attacks on their brothers and sisters in Dongyang, and they stopped attending the registered church. This infuriated the Three-Self leaders at Yiwu, and they too began persecuting the believers in that city.[3]

Although the persecution at Dongyang and Yiwu took place in one part of central Zhejiang, the repercussions for Christianity throughout the province were profound. Many believers dug their heels in and considered the offer to join the Three-Self Patriotic Movement a demonic ruse to destroy their churches. To this day, the majority of Christians in Dongyang and Yiwu continue to meet in unregistered meetings outside the control of the government, while in Xiaoshan County one report stated: "95 percent of the 63,000 Christians there belonged to the indigenous Little Flock group and are opposed to the TSPM, although showing every sign of being patriotic citizens in every other respect."[4]

# Doctor Jesus

The more the government tried to destroy the Church in Zhejiang, the more it multiplied, and during the 1980s numerous miracles occurred which displayed the matchless power and grace of Jesus Christ.

In one rural Zhejiang village a woman had suffered with a brain tumor for nine years. She had spent all of her money trying to fund a cure, but there was no improvement and she resigned herself to death. One day, as she lay in bed:

> The woman saw three people in white robes come into her house. They entered her room and one of them asked, "Do you want to be healed?"
>
> A white-robed man came near her and stroked her head where the tumor was. She felt fluid leaking from her head, and a lump being removed. Then the man seemed to close up the opening with a few quick movements of his fingers. The village woman instantly felt relieved. She asked, "What is your name, Doctor?" The white-robed man answered, "Jesus. You can find me in the nearest town." Then he disappeared.[5]

That evening the woman's children returned home from work, and she shared how a doctor had visited and given her free treatment. They paid little attention, thinking she was delirious.

The woman grew stronger every day, and the tumor had simply vanished. After a while she felt strong enough and set out for the neighboring town to thank Doctor Jesus for healing her. That day, a Christian grandmother in the town was taking care of her grandson. He was restless, so she decided to take him for a walk to use up some of his energy. As they walked out of their gate, the healed woman approached and asked where she could find the doctor named Jesus.

The grandmother took her to the local church, where the woman retold her story. The believers were not surprised, for miraculous healings were commonplace in those days. They told her who Jesus is and preached the gospel to her. She repented of her sins and returned home a new believer. Shortly after, "her whole family came to Christ. Her testimony quickly spread throughout her village, and many people wanted to believe in Jesus."[6]

## *The potato thief*

In Rui'an, south of Wenzhou, a Christian farmer had stacked his many potatoes outside his home, but someone kept stealing them, a few at a time. This brother decided he would stay up one night to see who the thief was. He concealed himself and waited all night. Finally the thief came, but before he took any potatoes he stopped and prayed out loud to heaven:

> O Spirit, please forgive me for coming again to steal these potatoes. I have come to the home of this Christian family because I know if they catch me they will not beat me, whereas if a non-Christian catches me they will beat me severely. Please forgive me, O heaven. You know that I have not come to take these potatoes for my own benefit, but that I need them to feed my starving family and newborn baby. Please forgive what I am about to do.[7]

When the Christian farmer heard the man's prayer he was heart-stricken. Tears welled up in his eyes as he realized he had not been attentive to his neighbor's needs.

After the thief completed his mission and returned home, the brother went inside and woke his wife, explaining what had happened. She was also deeply touched and they fell to their knees and repented of their selfishness.

The Christian couple decided to visit the thief and his family and bless them. They made up a basket of potatoes, sugar, flour, salt and other items as a gift. When they knocked on the door of his house, however, the thief refused to open it because he thought they had come to seek retribution and beat him.

After some time waiting outside, the Christians called out to the neighbor, "We have not come to punish you, but to seek your forgiveness. We have some gifts for you. Please open the door!"

This deeply touched the thief and his wife and children. The next day they told many other people in the village, "We stole the Christian family's food, yet *they* came to us and asked forgiveness!" Their testimony made a great impact on many people. Revival broke out in that village and dozens of families gave their lives to Jesus.

## *Visitors from Henan*

By the late 1980s, God's Spirit was being mightily poured out on the rural house church believers in provinces like Henan and Anhui. Millions of people turned to Christ, causing some of the leaders to visit Zhejiang to see how God was working there, and to seek ways in which their house church networks could cooperate.

Sister Ding Hei, a well-known house church leader and evangelist with the Fangcheng movement in Henan Province, recalled a visit she and her co-workers made to Zhejiang in 1989:

> Four of us traveled to Yueqing City, where a huge crowd gathered to hear us speak. We testified about what God was doing in other parts of the country, then we asked the sick to come forward for prayer and invited all believers to come and be filled with the Holy Spirit. At least 80 percent of the sick we prayed for raised their hands when asked if they had been healed. The blind saw and the lame walked. God did great things.
>
> While one of us was speaking, a crippled 15-year-old girl was brought to the platform. She was deformed and was less than one meter (three and a half feet) tall. After the sermon the

girl said she wanted to go to the toilet. People carried her there and waited for her to return, but when she came out she said something astonishing happened to her and she didn't need to be carried back! The Lord had healed her and she walked back to the meeting unaided. Furthermore, she had grown taller and was now a normal height!

Next we visited Yongjia County, where a woman was dying from four different types of cancer. Her daughter attended our meeting and many miracles occurred. Later that afternoon, the girl came to the house where we were staying and begged us to come to the hospital to pray for her mother.

We were in the midst of our meetings and were so busy that we couldn't go, but we wrote her mother's name on the palms of our hands and prayed for her. It was 3:15 p.m. when we prayed, and the girl said that her mother was completely healed of all cancer at 3:15 as she lay in her hospital bed. The very next day both the mother and daughter came to our meeting and testified to what God had done. They followed us to all of our meetings. Like hungry puppies they lapped up everything they could eat and drink from the Word of God.[8]

Brother Yun, in his well-known biography *The Heavenly Man*, also visited Zhejiang in 1989 after his second long imprisonment for the gospel. Yun recalled:

I was invited to lead special meetings in Wenzhou, and great miracles took place. The blind saw, the deaf heard, and the lame walked. People who desperately needed the Lord surrounded us. They even touched my clothes, hoping to receive healing from the Lord. Finally, it took six or seven strong coworkers to carry me away from the crowd and out of the meeting.[9]

## *A decisive decade*

As the 1980s drew to a close, believers in Zhejiang looked back in astonishment on a decisive decade in the history of

Christianity in the province. Ten years earlier the Church had still been struggling to emerge from the Cultural Revolution, but tremendous growth throughout the 1980s and a dramatic shift in religious policy meant that many believers could now come out of the shadows, both in government-approved Three-Self churches and in the new "registered house churches" of Wenzhou.

Christian estimates from Zhejiang throughout the 1980s provide a snapshot of the tremendous growth that had taken place. In 1984 an official source connected to the Three-Self Church gave the number of registered church members in the province as 700,000 believers in 1,200 churches.[10] The Three-Self, however, publishes notoriously conservative numbers that only take baptized adult church members into account.

Two years later, another Christian publication estimated a total of three million Evangelical believers in Zhejiang Province.[11]

During the 1980s, the church leaders in Zhejiang also started sending evangelists to other provinces. Before that time they had concentrated on the needs of their own people, but after the gospel had already spread to most parts of the province, they lifted up their eyes to needs further afield.

The Christians in northern Zhejiang were grieved to learn that a massive idol had been erected in a town across the border in neighboring Anhui Province. They flooded the town with evangelists, and their powerful preaching convinced many people to abandon their sins and false gods. Many pilgrims who traveled to view the idol threw their joss sticks on the ground and stomped on them.

The Communist Party appeared to view the upsurge of Christianity in Zhejiang with both bewilderment and anger. The more the nation's leaders had tried to suppress the Church, the stronger it had grown, and they appeared to be at a total loss as to what to do next. An official report in 1988 noted that many Party members had resigned their affiliation and become Christians. In Pingyang County, "108 Party members believed in Christianity. About half had believed because they or family members had met with sickness or other disasters and no-one in the Party had bothered to care for them."[12]

By the end of the 1980s it was apparent that not only had the Church in Zhejiang survived three decades of hardship and struggle, but thousands of flourishing churches had emerged, full of vibrant and joyful believers! In summarizing the revival in Zhejiang throughout the 1980s, veteran China missionary Leslie Lyall wrote:

> Hudson Taylor and his first party of pioneers settled in Hangzhou, the beautiful lakeside provincial capital. Officially there are 900,000 [registered] Christians in the province, meeting in 1,600 churches, but with only 300 pastors . . .
>
> In Hangzhou alone there are three registered churches and 700 additional meeting points. The Drum Tower Church holds three services each Sunday attended by about 3,000 people. Two-thirds of the members have become Christians during or since the Cultural Revolution. Eighty baptisms on a day is not uncommon . . .
>
> Wenzhou has become known as the "Jerusalem" or "Holy Land" of China. In one area of eight counties there are 330,000 Christians—in one village Christians are 80 percent of the population![13]

# Miao Zizhong—the Cedar of Lebanon

*Miao Zizhong*

On the night of October 17, 1989, more than a thousand tearful Christians gathered outside a small village in Wencheng County, a mountainous area southwest of the city of Wenzhou. As the brothers and sisters respectfully sang "Waiting for the Lord's Return to Meet Again," the body of Miao Zizhong was lowered into a grave. This man, who had gone to be with his Lord at the age of 73, was so highly respected that he had earned the nickname "the Cedar of Lebanon" from his fellow believers.

In the 1950s a total of 49 Chinese pastors from the Wenzhou area were arrested and sent to prison labor camps in northeast China's frozen Heilongjiang Province. Of these 49 men, Miao Zizhong was the only one to survive the ordeal and return home alive.

Miao was born in 1916, and grew up without knowing the gospel. Indeed he regularly hurled foul-mouthed insults at the servants of the Lord. He became an angry man, bitterly lashing out at other people without provocation.

Everything began to change in Miao's life in 1948, one year before China became a Communist country. When he was 32 he contracted a fatal disease, and when he went to the largest hospital in Wenzhou they declared his case incurable and advised him to return home and prepare for death. News got around that Miao was perishing, and a relative visited and pleaded with him to believe in Jesus Christ. He accepted the gospel and repented of his sins.

From the moment Miao received God's offer of salvation, his physical condition improved, and after a while he was completely healed. Overcome with gratitude to the Lord for sparing his life, Miao surrendered his future to serving Him, and he immediately traveled to another county to preach the gospel.

For the next six years Miao continued to proclaim the good news to the spiritually hungry people of Zhejiang, until the authorities finally caught up with him in the winter of 1954. He was hauled in front of a "struggle session" by the local people's militia, and was lectured about the evils of Christianity and commanded to sign a statement renouncing his faith. With a calm demeanor, Miao looked his persecutors in the eyes and declared:

"Jesus is the Savior of my life. I would be ungrateful to deny Him and as such I would go to hell. I cannot do this." Upon hearing that, the cadres began to gnash their teeth and with their fists they started beating Zizhong viciously. He prayed fervently, asking the Lord for help. The evil men used every method, but in the end were unable to coerce Zizhong into submission.[1]

Although he was permitted to return home that day, Miao was declared a "counter-revolutionary," and it was only a matter of time before the government officials decided what they would do to silence him. A few months later he was falsely charged with the crime of "collaborating with overseas counter-revolutionary organizations," and was sentenced to five years' reform through labor in Heilongjiang Province near the border with Russia.

Miao struggled with the bleak conditions and the incessant back-breaking work at the prison camp. He had no hope in this world, and reasoned that if he was destined to die in that place then he should die sharing the gospel with his fellow inmates. When the prison authorities discovered he was still propagating his faith, they flew into a rage and added ten years to his sentence.

## Miao's lowest point

The greatest difficulty Miao Zizhong experienced during his first year in prison was the bitterly cold winters in Heilongjiang. One day, a group of more than 70 elderly Christian prisoners were forced to walk to another place for work. To reach their destination, they had to cross a frozen river. When they reached the middle of the river the ice cracked from the combined weight of the men and they plunged into the frigid water. Although most of the men were able to scramble up the riverbank, their wet clothing soon caused all but one to die of hypothermia.

On one occasion, the cruel prison wardens tortured Miao by removing a heavy iron grate from the oven and hanging it around his neck. He was forced to parade around the prison courtyard with the grate—which weighed more than 40 pounds (20 kg)—dangling from his neck. When they had finished mocking him that day, Miao was placed in stocks and thrown into solitary confinement for several months.

Despite the intense beatings, loneliness and deprivation, Miao experienced his most difficult moment during his second year of incarceration. His wife back in Zhejiang had been his best friend and a faithful companion since their wedding, but one day the prison officials delivered a letter from her in which she requested a divorce. She had heard that Miao's sentence had been extended to 15 years, and at that point gave up all hope of seeing him alive again. She decided it was better to make a fresh start as a single woman.

Miao was in a state of shock after reading his wife's letter, and after her words sank in he became so angry that he fainted. He had reached his lowest point. Miao considered his miserable situation. Because of the offense of the cross, he now found himself in a heartless prison with his days dominated by:

> the prison guard's leather whip and endless "struggle" sessions. Back home he had no parents, nor a single brother or sister. His only hope had been the prayers of his wife and her words of comfort expressed in her letters, but this day she had heartlessly severed their relationship. He had lost the one person on earth who was close to him . . .

> Taking no notice of the cold, Miao opened the cell door and ran to a grove where he fell to his knees on the snow-covered ground. With loud sobs he wept before the Lord. He was unable

to suppress his grief and tears flowed like a fountain. Suddenly he heard a very clear, personal and tender small voice from heaven saying, "You must be patient that you may fulfil God's will and obtain the promise" . . . Miao poured out his heart to the Lord in song:

> *"My family has deserted me, my friends ridicule me*
> *Lord, my heart loves you.*
> *I patiently and humbly accept your reproach*
> *Lord, my heart loves you.*
> *Lord, my heart loves you.*
> *Let the oceans dry up and the stones be crushed*
> *Lord, my heart loves you."[2]*

Miao Zizhong received comfort and strength from the Holy Spirit as he emptied his soul before God, and he realized that Christ alone would never leave or forsake him. He returned to his cell and replied to his wife's letter, telling her to proceed with the divorce if she wished.

## *An angelic encounter*

The overcrowded prison camp was home to 1,300 men from across China, including many church leaders. The unhygienic conditions provided a fertile environment for disease. During one especially cold winter, when the temperature plummeted to minus 45° Celsius (-49° F), a plague swept through the labor camp. Within hours, hundreds of men had come down with severe fever. Their eyes bulged from their heads, and many went into convulsions and died. Bodies were dragged out of the cells and tossed into a giant pit, and within days 1,050 of the 1,300 men had perished.

Miao was also infected by the horrible plague and was taken to see a doctor, who shook his head and said, "Here is another one." He was put in a room where corpses were being stored before being taken out for burial. As Zizhong lay among many dead bodies he prayed:

> Lord, I ask you to save me. Please don't allow me to die here whereby your Name will be reproached. Heal me and allow me to return home in peace. I will serve you all the days of my life and do the work of an evangelist.[3]

Suddenly, an angel dressed in a glorious white robe appeared and tenderly said, "Do not fear. Only believe." In his own words, Miao Zizhong recalled what happened next as he teetered between life and death:

> The angel stretched out his right hand and took hold of my left hand and led me out of that building. I was taken to a beautiful room, pure white beyond description. The angel had me sit on a chair and he took a stethoscope from around his neck. He took a white tube and put it in my mouth. The angel blew into it and I felt a cool sensation which made me feel comfortable.
>
> When I came to, my sickness had left me. I knelt among the dead bodies and loudly praised the Lord. I again dedicated my whole life to Jesus. I went back to the doctor and asked for food. When the doctor saw me entering he was so shocked he broke into a cold sweat and stumbled backwards, crying out, "Are . . . you . . . a . . . ghost?"
>
> I laughed and said, "Don't be afraid. I am Miao Zizhong. My God has healed me and saved me from death. He has sent me to proclaim the way of salvation to you. Therefore you must believe in Jesus."
>
> Upon hearing that, the doctor immediately knelt down, saying, "Your God is true. Jesus is alive. I now believe and ask Jesus to receive me."[4]

## Return to trouble

The years went by, until Miao found himself the longest-serving inmate at the Heilongjiang labor camp. Thousands of men had come and gone, with even young prisoners only managing to survive a few weeks before they died. Yet through it all, Miao had endured, and his faith in Jesus Christ remained intact. One secret to his survival was that he often slipped away from his cell late at night when the other exhausted prisoners were asleep. He would go to a small grove on the compound where he knelt down and prayed to God, and the Holy Spirit always met him in that blessed place, giving him strength and encouragement to endure another day.

In 1969 Miao completed his 15-year sentence and was placed on a train back home to Zhejiang Province. He was unaware at the time, but his release came at the height of the Cultural Revolution, when Red Guards were terrorizing the land and Christians everywhere were under intense pressure. As soon as the local officials discovered that Miao had returned home, he was called in for questioning. When he was asked if the last 15 years had changed his religious beliefs, Miao Zizhong boldly replied, "These 15 years of labor reform have not changed my belief; moreover, my relationship with Jesus has been strengthened and my faith is stronger than ever!"[5]

Once again, this man of God's calm but clear answers infuriated his persecutors. They flew into a fit of rage, pushed him to the floor, and beat him with their fists and batons.

The following year Miao was ordered to attend re-education classes by the local authorities, along with dozens of criminals and gangsters. The evangelist continued to put Jesus first, and each time he lifted up his rice bowl to give thanks to God, the other men would grab the bowl from his hands and strike his head with a powerful blow.

One hot summer afternoon, the Red Guards came and bound Miao's hands tightly behind his back. He was dragged to a place where a high wooden platform had been erected. Officials accused him of "hideous crimes" he had supposedly committed against the nation. They commanded Miao to publicly deny Jesus, and finished by snarling, "Today, if you continue to believe in Jesus, we will beat you to death!"

Miao Zizhong had walked with God for many years by this time, and he was not going to throw away everything he had stood for. His life meant very little to him, but his faith and the presence of the Holy Spirit meant everything. He looked down from the platform at the large crowd that had gathered, and with a loud voice he made a speech which has gone down as a seminal moment in the annals of Christianity in Zhejiang. Miao declared:

> Fellow countrymen, because of belief in Jesus I have already spent 15 years in the Heilongjiang labor reform prison, where I was "struggled against" and beaten several times, yet my faith is stronger than ever. Why is that? It's because the Lord Jesus whom I believe in is the true and living God. He is the Son of God, the Creator of heaven and earth. He was born for us, and because of our sins He was crucified on the cross. Therefore all of you should repent, leave your idols, cease from violence and believe in Jesus that you may obtain eternal life.[6]

As soon as these words left Miao's lips a mob of brutal men rushed onto the platform, where they proceeded to kick and beat his head and entire body. As he slowly collapsed to the ground, his voice could be heard above the commotion, saying, "Lord, please forgive them. I commit my soul to You."

Miao was seriously injured. His ribs and other bones had been broken, and he was covered in welts and bruises. Tufts of hair had been ripped from his scalp. He slowly recovered, however, and several months later he was back preaching the gospel to those who were willing to hear.

During another public humiliation meeting later that year, Christians who were present testified that Miao's face shone with glory, like that of an angel. He even taunted his persecutors, who demanded to know the secret of his stubborn resistance, by telling them: "Why don't you bring out a knife and cut out my heart? Then you will know what's in it."

Countless more persecutions continued, including one episode when Miao was hit on the head with a small iron hammer after he refused to deny Christ. After several blows his head swelled to the size of a gourd, but his integrity and love for Jesus remained intact.

## *The final lap*

After all the abuse Miao Zizhong had endured over the years, people were sure he wouldn't live long, but the Spirit of Jesus helped him complete his race and finish the work entrusted to him. The authorities in Zhejiang didn't know what to do with this man. They had treated him with extreme violence, yet he continued to believe in God and encourage others to do the same.

Instead of persecuting Miao themselves, the local government officials hired a group of thugs to do their dirty work for them. As they dragged the man of God through the streets, they tortured him with knives and kicked him to the ground. When they passed a cesspool full of human waste, they threw Miao's hat into the muck, then retrieved it with a bamboo pole and placed it back on his head.

To howls of laughter, the excrement ran down his face and soaked his shirt. Then, according to an eyewitness:

one of the thugs . . . picked up a lump of dog excrement and stuffed it into Zizhong's mouth. He shut his mouth tight, but they smeared his mouth and lips with the smelly dog waste. Zizhong opened his mouth and began to spit it out, but all that came out were several mouthfuls of fresh blood.[7]

As Miao Zizhong aged into his sixties, many Christians wanted to know the secret to his victorious faith. One visitor shared insights into his daily routine:

> He would rise early each morning to intercede with weeping for the country, the people and the Church. Every morning after the time of prayer, he would put on his reading glasses and, under a small kerosene lamp, read the Bible. He would often not go to bed and even skipped meals to study the Bible. He put much effort into studying the Word . . . You could ask him the location of any verse in the Bible and he would tell you. However, he was not satisfied and very often humbly requested that the brethren teach him.
>
> Each time he received a revelation from the Bible, he would jump up and dance with great joy. He remained single after his wife divorced him. For years he lived a hard life in which he constantly traveled for the work of the Lord. He experienced much bitterness in this life. Even so, he was full of joy. In every home he stayed there was always the sound of singing. As he got older his voice was stronger than most young people. Often he would sing, cry and laugh until tears flowed.[8]

Finally, in October 1989, the 73-year-old Cedar of Lebanon fell, not to rise again until the resurrection of the dead. Miao Zizhong left behind no children, except the thousands of spiritual children he had led to the Lord and nourished with God's Word.

# 1990s

## Cycles of persecution and calm

The 1990s commenced with the growth of Christianity in Zhejiang continuing full steam ahead. With an estimated three million Evangelical believers in the province at the start of the decade, the Chinese government was deeply alarmed, especially when the churches started to send evangelistic teams to other parts of the country.

In a bid to counteract the expanding influence of the Zhejiang Church, the authorities took a variety of approaches, and the 1990s were characterized by fluctuating periods of intense

*Believers in Zhejiang gather for the funeral of a church member in the 1990s*

persecution, followed by times of calm. Christians learned to be watchful, discerning the latest season and adjusting their behavior accordingly.

Churches in Wenzhou City had enjoyed a relatively trouble-free existence since the mid-1980s, and had used the peaceful period to construct hundreds of new church buildings, some with elaborate designs resembling European cathedrals. Things were about to drastically change, however, and by the end of the decade hundreds of those same buildings had been bull-dozed to the ground by an angry government determined to keep the lid on Christianity.

The tide in Wenzhou unexpectedly turned in September 1991, during a large baptismal service attended by 2,000 Christians from several unregistered house churches. Witnesses said that during the meeting:

> A large band of Public Security officers suddenly stormed into the church and began firing pistols into the air. Some officers ran onto the platform and began beating the pastors who were conducting the service. Several pastors were arrested and taken to a detention center.
>
> House church Christians were surprised and angered by the unprovoked attack, which was conducted without search or arrest warrants. A large group of local Christians went to the Wenzhou Public Security Bureau to protest the assaults and arrests, but authorities there denied any knowledge of the incident . . . Several who were injured in the assault were left in poor condition.[1]

## Revival comes to the Three-Self

In the 1990s a new dynamic began to take place in Zhejiang, which caught both the authorities and many watchers of the China Church by surprise. The government had expended much time and energy trying to induce Christians to submit to the authority of the Three-Self Patriotic Movement, and many hundreds of congregations had registered. If the government assumed that the spiritual life and vitality of those churches would be contained, it was mistaken. The King of Kings refused to allow His blessings to be confined to just one type of believers in Zhejiang, and the wind of the Holy Spirit also began to blow powerfully on the Three-Self churches in the province. Revival broke out in many registered churches, accompanied by countless healings and other miracles, and the salvation of hundreds of thousands of people.

The Three-Self Church had notoriously reported low figures in Zhejiang—perhaps not wanting to alert government officials in Beijing to the true size and influence of the Church—but even those official sources revealed that the number of adult, baptized Three-Self church members in the province grew markedly from 900,000 in 1990[2] to 1.2 million in 1994[3] and 1.3 million in 1997.[4]

In addition, the Catholic churches in Zhejiang also grew at a startling rate. The previous reliable survey of Catholics in the province was conducted way back in 1937, showing a total of 100,236 believers in Zhejiang.[5] Finally, after a gap of more than half a century, the Chinese Academy of Social Sciences estimated that Catholics in the province had grown to 700,000 by 1992.[6]

## *Revival comes to the Little Flock*

The Little Flock was founded by Watchman Nee (Ni Tuosheng). It expanded into Zhejiang in the 1930s and flourished, especially in northern parts of the province. The official name for this church movement is the Local Church, but many Christians came to call it "the Little Flock" as its congregations used a hymn book called "Hymns for the Little Flock."

The government was confused as to why the movement exhibited such strength and unity among its members, and in 1995 a scholar from the Center for Ethnological Studies was dispatched to Huzhou Prefecture in a bid to understand the phenomenon. His report was most revealing:

> Between 1982 and 1989 the number of Christians in the Huzhou region increased six-fold to about 25,000 . . . We visited villages inhabited by the Little Flock . . . They admit they are not as well educated as Christians in southern Zhejiang, where Christianity has a history of over a century compared to only ten years in their district. But "grace grows from suffering", and they proudly told us that their spiritual development is higher than those living in materially better-off regions. In all simplicity they believe in the power of prayer and that one must "in all things pray".
>
> While praying, they experience the filling of the Spirit who guides their every word and action. In order that someone is healed, several (and sometimes dozens) of villagers will assemble for days of prayer and fasting . . .
>
> Originally, the Little Flock in Huzhou was part of the TSPM, but in 1985, because of many differences, they decided to separate. Today their suspicions and lack of trust in the Three-Self are shown by their belief that Jesus is the Head of the Church, not any man. The Church should not be led by the government, but the TSPM churches . . . are arrogant, ignorant of the Scriptures, and not rigorous enough in morality . . .
>
> In Xiaoshan City near Hangzhou there are 80,000 Christians, of whom 70,000 belong to the Little Flock. They believe their patriotism should be shown in their work-places and not in church, so they refuse to join the Three-Self Patriotic Movement.[7]

With such a strong foundation in the Scriptures and zeal for God's work, it's not surprising that believers from the Little

Flock congregations in Zhejiang began to send missionaries to unreached areas of China. Starting in January 1991, many members of the Little Flock felt that the return of Christ was imminent. As a result:

> After earnest prayer, several went to Guangxi and Hunan provinces to preach. Soon they returned with the good news that several dozen people had been converted. This electrified dozens of house churches in Xiaoshan who caught the vision to evangelize. In each church between six and several dozen young Christian men were sent out. Most were farmers, and the mainstay of their families, but they gladly sacrificed their work-time and income to preach the gospel. They set off in pairs in March 1991 for Hunan, Shandong, Jiangsu, Sichuan and other places all over China. Those left at home were fully behind the young evangelists. They set up 24-hour prayer chains with 12 bands of prayer warriors each praying for two hours every day.[8]

The success of the Little Flock missionaries was extraordinary. A report from Xiaoshan in May 1991 said:

> It seemed that the brothers just had to open their mouths to speak and people would express a desire to receive Christ. One pair of preachers after just a few days reported that 300 people had turned to Christ. When the two dozen evangelists from one house church returned, they reported that 1,300 people had received salvation. This was the power of God, as how else could so few cause more than 1,000 people to believe?
>
> Young evangelists from another church had never preached like this before, so when they arrived at their destination they knelt down and prayed fervently. Then they preached to the bystanders and on the first day, 40 believed. On the second day more than 200 turned to Christ . . .
>
> By the end of May 1991, most of the evangelists had returned to Zhejiang. Although no direct count was made, they estimated

that over 10,000 people had been saved as a result of this two-month evangelistic outreach. The house churches in Xiaoshan continued to send workers to do pastoral and follow-up work. Older, more experienced brethren were also dispatched to conduct baptisms and to oversee the establishment of churches.[9]

## *Growing pains*

Miracles continued to occur regularly throughout Zhejiang as the gospel was proclaimed in the 1990s. Unlike in some parts of the world, where only ordained ministers are expected to pray for the sick, in Zhejiang even young children preached the gospel and saw the Holy Spirit move powerfully. In a village near Hangzhou:

> An eight-year-old Christian boy was playing with his young neighbor when the latter unwittingly poked him in the eye with a sharp bamboo spike. The boy lost the sight in his left eye, and he and his family were so grief-stricken that they were, at first, unable to forgive their neighbor. However, through prayer they were filled with a spirit of forgiveness and over several weeks the boy's eyesight returned. The whole village was amazed at his unexpected recovery, and many accepted Jesus as their Savior because of this testimony.[10]

In another part of Zhejiang, a man with a serious heart disease had spent all of his money on medicine, but his condition had gradually worsened. One day he heard that whoever believes in Jesus Christ will have eternal life. Knowing he would soon die, by faith he asked someone to drive him to a believer's home. After hearing the gospel, he repented of his sins and surrendered his life to God.

The Christians took turns praying fervently for him throughout the night, and seven days later the man felt that God had healed him. He returned home and made his house available as a meeting place for God's people. Because of this, 90 percent of the people in that village turned to Christ, and within weeks he had 200 people meeting regularly in his home.

Despite the many evidences of God's grace and mercy being poured out among the people of Zhejiang, the Church faced many large and important challenges. The most desperate need was the lack of trained Bible teachers in their midst, which threatened to derail the revival in its tracks.

With even the government-controlled churches growing strongly, a massive shortage of trained church leaders arose throughout the province. Rural house church meetings often took place without a leader, and preachers were asked to travel around a group of villages and towns holding meetings, which believers were encouraged to attend. This chronic shortage of leaders, coupled with a low rate of literacy in the countryside and a lack of Bibles, created a toxic cocktail which resulted in many thousands of professing believers falling away from the faith. The void in solid biblical teaching also gave rise to cults and heresies. One report highlighted the seriousness of the problem:

> Simplistic and literal interpretations of the Scriptures have led to cases of women attempting to sacrifice their sons in an imitation of the Old Testament account of Abraham and Isaac. In blind faith, others have drowned as they attempted to walk on water as Jesus did.
>
> The yearning for the Second Coming of Christ brought its share of problems. One church in Zhejiang predicted Jesus would return on April 18, 1991. Farms and crops were abandoned and animals were slaughtered and eaten . . . April 18 passed, leaving the confused and disillusioned group of men and women on a hillside, gazing heavenward.[11]

## The storm of 1997

Incredibly, the "registered house church" phenomenon in Wenzhou had mushroomed to such an extent that by the mid-1990s more than 2,400 congregations in the city had registered as independent churches. Some had seating capacity for several thousand people.

Indications that the government's tolerance of Christianity in Wenzhou was coming to an end surfaced in April 1996, when a house church believer in his mid-forties was arrested near Wenzhou for illegally printing Christian literature. He was beaten to death by the Public Security Bureau. Two other men were sentenced to three years in prison.[12]

In early 1997, Chinese President Jiang Zemin visited Wenzhou, and was apparently shocked by the enormous number of church buildings in the city, each adorned with a red cross on the roof. For a man who had first joined the Communist Party as a college student and had risen up the ranks during Mao's rule and the excesses of the Cultural Revolution, such a bold display of religious faith was humiliating and intolerable.

Later that year the Religious Affairs Bureau was directed to cut down the profile of Christianity in the city. In one six-week period in November and December, more than 400 church buildings were bulldozed to the ground throughout Wenzhou. During the demolition process more than 50 pastors were arrested. The persecution quickly spread to other house churches throughout Zhejiang, with one pastor reporting:

> The angry waves attacking the Chinese Church have grown higher and higher. Since March this year we have been engulfed and the Church has entered a period of intense suffering. Many leaders have been arrested, especially in Wenzhou, Rui'an, and Yongjia (in southern Zhejiang), and in Cixi, Ninghai and

181

*Before and after pictures of Wenzhou's Christ Church, one of 400 churches in the city demolished by the government in 1997*
VOM

Dongtou (northern Zhejiang). Some have suffered physical pain. Whole families have had to flee. Just in the town of Tangxia in Rui'an County, 32 house church leaders have been arrested. Others have fled the area.

The persecution is even worse than during the Cultural Revolution. At least then they searched homes while the head of the household was present. Now they smash down doors and ransack homes even when the owner is away. They come in police cars, sirens blaring, and surround Christians' homes as if they were robbers, arresting them as "counter-revolutionaries" . . . Please pray urgently. I am on the arrest list and have had to leave home.[13]

The storm of persecution slowly passed over Zhejiang Province, as the government shifted its attention to other matters. At the start of 1998, however, dozens of Christian leaders remained in prison and tens of thousands of believers in Wenzhou had seen their places of worship reduced to rubble.

## Missionaries meet resistance

The 1990s saw the first serious attempt by Zhejiang house churches to send missionaries to other parts of China and even to other countries. Wenzhou believers gladly took the lead, using their wealth and experience gained as entrepreneurs to spearhead the effort. In 1996 a church leader summarized the different stages of growth that the body of Christ in Wenzhou had gone through to reach that stage:

The revival in the 1970s initiated the present church growth in our area. In the 1980s a lot of people gathered in houses, sometimes over 200 people in one house. As a result we started to build church buildings in each area . . .

This decade is characterized by evangelism and mission efforts outside of our province. Now, our church sends evangelists to other provinces such as Heilongjiang, Henan, Hunan, Guangxi, Yunnan, Anhui and Jiangxi. We send our workers to these provinces every year. This year we have sent 40 and the results are extremely good. For example, in Jiangxi, 169 people were baptized . . .

We send our people to where pioneer work is needed. If weak churches need our help we are willing to go and help them develop. For example, in early 1995 we sent workers to Heilongjiang and pioneered 18 new churches in areas where there weren't any. But we also helped 38 existing churches. One of them had only about ten Christians to start with, but since our workers went there the congregation has grown to over 200.[14]

By the mid-1990s the Wenzhou churches had sent missionaries to the ethnic minority groups living along China's borders with Myanmar and Russia, and had mission teams ministering in several foreign countries, including Thailand and Vietnam.

Predictably, many of the Wenzhou missionaries experienced persecution as they took the gospel to previously unreached areas of China, but they were also surprised to encounter resistance from some of the house church Christians in other parts of the country. The massive house church networks in Henan Province, which by then numbered millions of believers, struggled to accept the Wenzhou evangelists. They differed in doctrine and practice, and even the linguistic differences between Wenzhou and the rest of China created misunderstandings.

The resistance experienced by the Wenzhou workers appears to have been primarily cultural and social. Wenzhou Christians are generally highly educated, successful at business and well-dressed. In Henan, however, the mighty revival that had swept millions into God's kingdom was largely among poor, illiterate farmers. Although each side acknowledged one another as fellow believers in Christ, no close working relationship was formed.

Peter Xu Yongze, the founder of the large Born-Again Movement, candidly shared his unflattering impressions of Wenzhou believers at that time. He opined:

> The Wenzhou Church has a lot of spiritual pride. They see themselves as the heart and soul of the Church in China, and can never accept that there are more believers in provinces like Henan and Anhui than there are in their area.[15]

Sister Ding Hei, a well-known evangelist with the Fangcheng house church network, also based in Henan, echoed these concerns about the Wenzhou Christians. When she was asked her thoughts on the government's demolition of hundreds of churches in Wenzhou, she replied:

> I believe this was the will of God. I have seen that most of the churches in Wenzhou are filled with pride. In 1981 I visited there for the first time, and have returned almost every year since. In the early years the Wenzhou churches experienced the Lord's blessing in a mighty way, but in recent years they have become legalistic and performance-orientated. They appear to be very open to the Lord but in reality they look down on pastors from Henan and consider themselves better than others. The leaders often point at us and say, "You Henan leaders are uneducated. How can you come to teach us? We have been Christians for more than a century. You should come and learn from us."
>
> In my experience, many of the Wenzhou pastors are good men who love the Lord. The teaching in the church is good and accurate, but they receive no vision from the Lord. They have the basics correct, but they have no power. Not receiving vision from the Lord is the worst kind of suffering a Christian can experience.
>
> Many of the Christians in Wenzhou are wealthy businessmen, so they have used their money to build expensive church buildings. I see the destruction of their church buildings as God's chance for them to get back to the basics of following Him

again. The Wenzhou Church will survive, but not their build-ings. If the Wenzhou believers had the same kind of suffering as we have in Henan, the growth of the gospel would double throughout China.[16]

## *Letters from Zhejiang*

We conclude this chapter by reprinting a selection of letters that were received from Zhejiang by various Christian minis-tries during the 1990s. These precious communications reveal both the strengths and weaknesses of Christianity in Zhejiang, and provide insights into the daily lives and personal struggles of believers as they followed God. Their experiences offer a fas-cinating snapshot of the ever-changing conditions experienced by the body of Christ at this time.

### 1991

I have two children, aged 12 and seven. Three years ago my husband left home on a business trip and never returned. He is still wandering and leading an indecent life. He has written me twice saying he is never going to return and that I should prepare for a divorce. I don't know what to do. Who is going to accept my two children if I marry again? If I arrange for someone to look after them, I'm afraid my husband will create trouble. It's difficult for me to go on like this.[17]

### 1992

I am 34 years old and was raised an atheist. I didn't know anything about God; but praise the Lord, I was saved during an illness last year. At first I didn't understand the Scriptures.

My spiritual life and knowledge of God was shallow. I was only looking for His might and power because of my sickness. I couldn't see my need for God's gracious salvation, but He did not reject me. The Lord loved me and saved my life. Now He helps and strengthens me both physically and spiritually each day, and I have given my body and soul to God without reservation.[18]

I am a high school student and also a member of the Communist Youth League. According to the law, a member cannot have any religious affiliation. Although I am not a fully committed Christian, I do not doubt the existence of God and His power. Should I resign from the Party? If I quit, I will be accused by my teachers and fellow students. It will also influence my future study and work. What shall I do?[19]

## 1995

I have been troubled about whether or not I should join the Communist Youth League. I know that as a Christian, I am a child of God. Thus, joining an atheist organization is absolutely incompatible with my identity. However, my teachers have given me strong recommendations and my classmates have nominated me to become a member. My mind is filled with self-reproach for not being willing to give up such a minor thing for God. How can I be loyal to God in important matters if I am not loyal in trivial ones?[20]

Preparing and preaching sermons nowadays is a difficult task for me. An elderly preacher taught us from John 5 about the healing at the pool of Bethesda. He said there were three truths in the text about baptism. I took down his words and started giving the same message, but I was not at peace so I consulted two other preachers who told me my sermon was correct. However, when I asked three young servants of God, they said I was in error because the text does not describe baptism at all. I felt very bad because I had taught a false message. I have a deep pain inside and I don't want to preach any more sermons.[21]

## 1996

An officer from the local police station came on a motorcycle to arrest me and take me to the station for interrogation. At the time I was anxious but God gave me peace. On the way, I asked the officer what crime I had committed. He replied, "You know very well. At the police station you will have to confess everything!" Once there, it became clear they knew I had written a letter to a Christian organization in Hong Kong. Suddenly everything made sense. My letter had been opened by the customs and forwarded to the police for investigation. I thank God I live in Wenzhou where there is a great Christian revival. Please pray for me.[22]

## 1997

Here in Wenzhou some government officials are now preventing young people from believing in Christ. Our Sunday school has been dispersed, but we still worship in churches every Sunday.

Although we have suffered one attack after another, our love for the Lord has not changed. Many places throughout China are also suffering persecution. Please pray we will not lose faith and that the gospel will spread throughout the whole world.[23]

## 1998

I like studying but I failed the university entrance examination. I took the self-study test in hope of becoming a university graduate . . . After a year of study I encountered many problems. First, since the teachers are recruited from outside, some of them require us to have lessons on Sundays. As such, I cannot attend Sunday church services. My time and effort are limited and I cannot satisfy both . . . I have little faith. Please pray for me.[24]

I just graduated from university and have been teaching for a year. I have gradually trusted in the Lord Jesus, but due to a shortage of material, I cannot understand more about Him. There are lots of phrases I don't understand. I have been to the church to look for a Bible but never got anywhere. There are not many believers here and the churches are small. Most Christians don't have Bibles and don't understand the grace and power of the Lord. I hope you can send a Bible to me.[25]

The area north of Xiaoshan City is a land flowing with milk and honey. The economy is prospering, communications are modern, and people are well off. More importantly, the churches have been greatly revived. In our village of 2,000 people there are four meeting points. We belong to the Little Flock (founded by Watchman Nee) and strictly obey the Bible. As Christ is our Head, we reject government control of the Church. Consequently we often experience friction with the government.[26]

# 2000s

## Sunday schools targeted

Christianity in Wenzhou continued to flourish into the new millennium. At the start of the decade, an overview of just the government-approved Three-Self churches in the province noted:

> At present the whole of Zhejiang has 2,600 churches and 3,300 meeting points. There are over 1.4 million believers . . . About 70,000 people are added to the church and tens of thousands of revival meetings are held each year. The prosperity of the churches in Wenzhou and Hangzhou is most prominent . . .
>
> The Church in Wenzhou is growing very fast. There are over 700,000 believers there. The ratio of Christians to the

*A boy standing in front of a painting at a Wenzhou Sunday school*

population in this region is as high as 1:10. There are over 2,000 churches and a similar number of meeting points. No wonder the region is known as the Jerusalem of China. One of the characteristics of the Church in Wenzhou is the development of Sunday schools for children. The Church is very serious about ministry for children. Many of the believers were converted when they were little children because of the influence of their Christian parents . . .

As the number of Christians increases much faster than the number of pastors in China, there is a severe lack of shepherds to guide the flocks.[1]

For many years the Three-Self Patriotic Movement had enforced a policy that no person under the age of 18 could be baptized or receive religious instruction. The independent fellowships of Wenzhou, however, were not bound by that policy and they continued to vigorously train children to follow the Lord. Many of these youngsters then attended state schools during the week, where they witnessed to their classmates and even to their teachers.

The dichotomy between the policies of the Religious Affairs Bureau and the Zhejiang churches was rapidly nearing a confrontation. It arrived in the summer of 2002 when the authorities ordered all churches to stop instructing children under the age of 18. The government assumed that pastors would be unwilling to risk prosecution, but they were wrong. Starting at Wenzhou and radiating out to other parts of the province, church leaders openly defied the policy and continued to hold Sunday schools and other youth activities. Several churches even held large children's Bible camps, where thousands came to study the Scriptures.

With the threat of arrest hanging over their heads, Wenzhou's Christian leaders used their influence and took the case to the highest levels of power in Beijing. They argued there was no official law in China prohibiting children from engaging in religious activities, but that a policy had been created by the Religious Affairs Bureau without the backing of the law.

Even Bishop Ding Guanxun, the head of the Three-Self Patriotic Movement at the time, supported the Wenzhou church leaders in their bid to end the arbitrary persecution. The Wenzhou Religious Affairs Bureau, not wanting to argue the matter in court, backed down from implementing its policy and the churches continued training their future generations of leaders.

In December 2002 the *Washington Post* reported on the standoff in Wenzhou, saying:

> After six weeks of the crackdown, the government consented to a meeting with church officials from several districts on July 27. Church officials presented the government with six points, including complaints that churches had been closed illegally, that police and other government officials had overstepped their authority, and that nowhere in Chinese law did it stipulate that minors could not be involved in religion.
>
> The last point was the most explosive . . . "We said there are 13-year-old monks in China who are respected, why can't you have young Christians?" a participant in the meeting recounted. "The government didn't have anything to say. They knew we knew the law" . . .
>
> But the fight, it turned out, was not over. The government took the fight into the elementary schools, warning children not to attend Sunday school and banning government teachers from teaching there, cutting their salaries and stopping their promotions if they did.
>
> "We've asked the teachers in elementary schools to persuade their students not to go to church, and we talked to parents as well," said Xiang Yuenian, a Wenzhou Religious Affairs official. "We don't have strong or clear law to support us, so it's hard to do this job . . . But we must take strong measures to stop such

*A huge church in Wenzhou where thousands of children were trained in Sunday schools*

schools. We must take compulsory means to stop such wrong-doing!" . . .

The government also demanded that each church fill out a form listing all activities for 2003, saying that from now on each activity must get approval. "We're not going to fill this thing in," said the chief pastor at one Wenzhou church. "If they want to fight us, we will fight them. Jesus is on our side."[2]

## *The unique Wenzhou mission strategy*

The Wenzhou Church had developed differently from churches elsewhere in China. Many Christians in the city were wealthy, with even some billionaires (in US dollar terms) known to be numbered among the believers there. Because of Wenzhou's reputation as a prosperous city, hundreds of thousands of migrant laborers flocked to the city from throughout China. Seizing the opportunity, Christian factory owners used their resources to help spread the gospel. From the start:

The Church in Wenzhou paid much attention to those laborers, holding evangelistic outreach meetings just for them and providing transportation and meals for these meetings. Believers who are employers made efforts to encourage their employees to attend such meetings, even counting their attendance in the payroll.

The gospel rapidly spread to laborers from other regions, and many have become believers. When the converts return to their hometowns, they take the gospel with them. The Wenzhou churches then send workers to visit them and help build them up.[3]

Many Christians from Wenzhou received a vision from God to preach the gospel in remote ethnic minority areas of China, and they often proved to be rugged and effective evangelists. In 2001 a letter was received from a member of the previously unreached Shui minority in Guizhou Province, which said:

Our church is located in a remote place and transportation is inconvenient. However, the good servants of the Lord have gone to the trouble of traveling a long distance from Zhejiang to this impoverished and destitute place where the Shui minority group lives, in order to share the gospel with us. The brothers didn't mind climbing mountains and wading across rivers. They got blisters on their feet, but they never complained. In a remote and backward place like Guizhou, they willingly endured hard work and planted many churches.[4]

By the start of the new millennium, Chinese Christians found it easier to obtain passports, and many Wenzhou believers used their extraordinary entrepreneurial skills to travel throughout Asia, and to far-flung corners of the globe, where they engaged in both macro and micro business enterprises.

Hundreds of individual Wenzhou natives—ranging from restaurant owners to souvenir and peanut sellers—dispersed throughout the world. Journalist David Aikman recalls being in Barcelona, Spain, in the early 2000s, and having a friendly wager with a colleague that within 50 feet (15 meters) of any cathedral in Europe he would find a Chinese Christian from Wenzhou selling something. The following day they went to the door of the famous La Seu cathedral and located three Wenzhou believers plying their trade nearby!

Dozens of churches were established throughout Europe with a threefold purpose: they were designed first to cater to the spiritual needs of Wenzhou believers far from home; second, to reach other Chinese migrants; and third, to act as bases for outreach to the general populations. In addition to at least two dozen Wenzhou church communities in France, Italy, Spain and the United Kingdom, Aikman was told about:

> large communities of Wenzhou Chinese in Khabarovsk, Russia; Bucharest, Romania; and Budapest, Hungary . . . Wenzhou business families were often called "the Jews of China," for wherever they went they usually succeeded in undercutting and even driving out the non-Wenzhou Chinese . . . Everywhere the retail merchants went, it seemed, at least since the 1980s, they also started churches.[5]

## The storms of 2000 and 2001

In 1997 the government of China had launched a blistering attack on church buildings throughout the Wenzhou area, bulldozing more than 400 to the ground.

If the authorities had thought the 1997 campaign would send shockwaves through the Zhejiang Church, they gravely underestimated the tenacity of the body of Christ. The believers

*One of more than 1,000 church buildings that were destroyed, banned or confiscated by the government in 2000 and 2001*
VOM

in Wenzhou and throughout the province were not dismayed, and they soon resumed their passion for constructing places of worship.

After a few years of relative calm, an even larger campaign of destruction was launched against churches in Zhejiang in late 2000. The *Wenzhou Daily* newspaper revealed that:

> Between mid-November and December 5, 2000, 256 churches were destroyed, 153 banned and 19 confiscated in Ouhai District; 527 churches were destroyed, 35 banned and 74 confiscated in Cangnan County; 4 churches were destroyed and 4 confiscated in Wencheng County; and 9 churches were banned in Taishun County.[6]

In total, 1,081 church buildings were destroyed or closed down during just a few weeks of mayhem. Unlike the 1997 persecution, when the authorities had preferred the use of bulldozers to wreak havoc, this time their preference was to simply dynamite churches to the ground.

## *The gospel continues to blaze*

Despite the strong assault on the Zhejiang churches, the revival continued to burn in the hearts of men and women throughout the province. The authorities may have successfully reduced buildings to rubble and closed down many fellowships, but they were unable to prevent the Holy Spirit moving as He pleased in people's hearts, filling the spiritual void that more than half a century of Communism had created.

In 2007, after a decade of persecution had failed to halt the progress of the gospel, one source reported: "In Zhejiang Province a large-scale Christmas evangelistic meeting attracted more than 10,000 people! Two thousand people reportedly expressed a desire to accept Christ."[7]

Jesus Christ continued to prove irresistible for multitudes of people throughout Zhejiang. Hundreds of thousands continued to press into the kingdom of God each year, often because of dramatic answers to prayer. Miracles occurred not only among the poor and downtrodden of society, but also in high places.

The head of the Zhejiang Chamber of Commerce suffered from diabetes and terminal cancer, and was afraid he would soon die. On the recommendation of a Christian member of the Chamber, he traveled to Shanghai to see a pastor named Rong who was known to pray for the sick and see many of them recover. After several visits to Rong's house for prayer, the man noticed he was substantially better, and doctors finally declared him free of both cancer and diabetes!

The man was a well-known business leader in his region, and a member of the Communist Party. As a result of his healing, "he decided to become a Christian and is now very open about his newfound Christian faith, frequently sharing how God healed him in answer to prayer with his associates in the Chamber of Commerce!"[8]

## *Brutality in Xiaoshan*

The hostility displayed by the government against the body of Christ in Zhejiang was by no means confined to Wenzhou. Believers were regularly arrested, beaten and fined throughout the province, but in 2006 a series of particularly brutal and shameful attacks on Christians took place in the Xiaoshan District near Hangzhou.

The worst of these incidents occurred on the afternoon of July 29, at the site of a half-finished church building which had been entirely financed by local believers to serve 5,000 church members. The site originally housed a church that had been constructed in 1921. The building was seized by the Communists in the 1950s, before finally being returned three decades later. For a time the congregation met in an old rented building, but when an opportunity presented itself to buy the land and construct a new place of worship, the believers gave generously and the building commenced.

Hundreds of local Christians gathered at the site that afternoon to pray and worship God, with many elderly church members sitting on plastic chairs surrounding the construction site.

According to *Time* magazine, at about 2:30 p.m. four bulldozers and hundreds of trucks packed with officers drove to the location. Suddenly:

Thousands of uniformed police and plainclothes security officers appeared at the construction site. The authorities then demolished the church. Witnesses say police bludgeoned people indiscriminately with nightsticks. "They were picking up women—some of them old ladies—by the hair and swinging them around like dolls, then letting them crash to the ground," says a man who watched the clash from across the street . . .

The Xiaoshan District government described the scene differently, claiming that about 100 Christians "attacked and injured government officials" and that although the police detained a few protestors, none were injured. But a volunteer interviewed by *Time* produced receipts from the local hospital attesting to his treatment for broken ribs which he says many others suffered as well. "They treated us like dead dogs. Some of them scoffed as we lay there saying, 'Where is your God now? If you want to go to heaven, we'll help you get there right now.'"[9]

In the aftermath of the brutal and unprovoked attack in Xiaoshan, about 50 believers remained in prison without being formally charged, and several women were in great physical pain as a result of the cowardly beatings they had received. One woman, Wang Aizhen, remained hospitalized with broken chest bones. Most troubling was that several young students could not be found after the incident. They appear to have been taken away to a secret location and tortured.

## A decade of struggle and growth

The first decade of the twenty-first century concluded with the government of China seemingly incapable of stopping the growth of the Church in Zhejiang. The unregistered house churches in the province were continuing to soar in number, and even the government-sanctioned Three-Self churches were experiencing explosive growth.

Revival was the opposite of what the Communists had planned for, but they were powerless to stop it. Their only response was to lash out, dynamiting church buildings and

*The congregation of the main Three-Self church in Ningbo*
RCMI

beating Christians. The more they tried to crush the Church, the larger it grew, and the stronger the faith and determination of God's people became.

By the end of the decade the number of Christians in many cities and counties of Zhejiang was approaching 20 percent of the population. An internal government study lamented that even though Zhejiang was one of the smallest provinces in China, approximately one tenth of all Christians in China lived within the province.

The 2001 edition of the respected prayer guide *Operation World* estimated a total of 4.8 million Evangelical Christians in Zhejiang.[10] The decade of 2000–9 ended with a growing sense that the atheist government had reached an impasse with the Church in the province, and one side or the other was likely to gain the upper hand in the long struggle between the forces of light and darkness.

# Letters from Zhejiang

My grandfather led our rural church. He was one of the first group of 40 evangelists in the Wenzhou region. He died last October, aged 95, having given his entire life to the ministry of the gospel. The Holy Spirit was upon him. He evangelized so well that now we have eight churches. All are working together harmoniously for the Lord. It is true revival . . . My father is a retired teacher and is an overseer of the churches. Not only does he have to arrange all the preaching and pastor the flock, he also oversees everything else.

The church members are very scattered as this is a poor mountain area, and it stretches to some offshore islands 100 km [62 miles] away. Every time my father goes to preach he has to take food and gifts for the old people. His health is not good and three years ago he had a major operation . . . I long to be able to give up my job and study the Bible so I can help my father in the ministry.[11]

I am a freshman at university. For my age, I should be quite mature. Yet what is meant by maturity? Is it to lie, to take advantage of others or to do empty talk? My peers are doing this. It appears that this is the way of society. Yet this is not my style. As I am not talkative, I am often left behind. What should I do? Should I follow their path or stay on my own?[12]

# 2001

I am learning to serve the Lord. In 1998 we established a youth fellowship. Praise God, He set us apart from this sinful world so we did not spend all our time on the dance floor or playing computer games. Every time we meet the Holy Spirit works powerfully in our midst and we are filled with joy. Many of our young people are making great spiritual progress. The church leaders are very happy, too, but the temptations of this world are great, especially in this region of economic growth. It is difficult for young people to stand firm, so we are praying fervently.[13]

Some of our church members are confused by the Eastern Lightning cult, and some of our leaders have adopted strange teachings and extreme behaviors. They emphasize singing and reading the Bible, but they do not allow us to do other things at church.[14]

We live in a rural area. Our church was established not long ago and already we have five meeting points with more than 100 members. Most of our members are old grandmas and impoverished people. Few are young or middle-aged, and none are very enthusiastic. The farmers' lives are so busy that they do not even attend Sunday services regularly. Their spiritual lives are weak and fragile. This causes great difficulties. If people are available in the daytime, we gather then. If not, we meet in the evenings. Please teach us what to do.[15]

My church has a congregation of 500–600 members, of whom 400–500 are sisters. Not many of the brothers are spiritually gifted, and there is no discipleship training. Every year we baptize more than 30 new believers into the church, but at the same time there are ten or more who leave. They begin to love the world and are not allowed to take Communion because of sin. Most of our members are spiritually weak or newly baptized. Our incompetent pastor is restricted by his lack of knowledge and poor spiritual life. He sees the fragile spiritual lives of the congregation, but his ability is not equal to his ambition. There is no training of young men to carry on the ministry.[16]

## 2002

Today is an age of upheavals and fast-changing technology. Everyone turns to money with a manic obsession. I have experienced an ample life but also that of poverty. Thank the Lord, neither riches nor poverty has any impact, because His grace is sufficient for me. The most touching thing in my life is to know God and to be His child. My brightest treasure is God and my greatest satisfaction comes from glorifying Him with my words and deeds. However dark and corrupted this age may become, and how deeply money is loved, I will not follow after them. I want to be the salt and light of my society, to show forth the glory of my Lord and bring more people to Him.[17]

I am 21 years old and it should be the best time of my life. However, I am tortured by sickness and all my days are difficult and long. I was once very healthy but, at the age of 14,

I suddenly contracted an illness in my head, chest, abdomen, and the joints of my limbs. I was in great pain and sorrow when dealing with this hopeless situation.

One day a Christian in our village came to my home to borrow something. He was shocked to see me lying in bed and asked what had happened. I told him how I had gone through two operations and I needed to stay in bed. He preached the gospel and asked me to believe in the Lord. After discussion with my parents, I confessed Christ last October. Many brothers and sisters have visited and prayed for me after my conversion. They teach me how to read the Bible and pray, and they take me to church on Sundays. My whole life has become better, although my neck vertebrae and right leg are giving me problems again and I think I need another operation. I really don't know what to do.[18]

At school I was really powerless to overcome my weakness, and I felt deep drowsiness every time class was in progress. A friend gave me a booklet entitled, "Knowing the True God." Thank God that He helped me read it through and I knelt next to my bed and prayed the prayer in the back of the booklet. Amazingly, the next day I began to sing out loud with great joy in my heart. My friend took me to a church meeting where I felt a strong power inside of me, and now I have fellowship with other sisters in the church and I feel the love of God.[19]

## 2005

We meet in a Christian brother's home. Recently, people from the Three-Self Church came and told us we had to join their movement. Our church consists of middle-aged and elderly men and women, and there is not the slightest benefit for us in joining the Three-Self. Moreover, everybody has a bad feeling about the Three-Self. They have said they will come and forcibly interfere with our church. When our members heard this they all felt worried. We fear our church will not be able to continue.[20]

# 2006

There is no mission department in my church. I was so touched by the Lord that I want to go to Mongolia to carry out mission work, but I am at a loss as to how to begin. I feel overwhelmed by the scale of the undertaking and feel that doing this by personal effort will not take me very far. I have held back, but I find this unbearable too.[21]

Last year the Public Security came to my school looking for me, but I was away. A Christian sister said they will come looking for me at work. When fear came upon me, through prayer God granted me great peace. Up until now the police have not found me. The fellowship I attended at university is facing persecution. Our meetings now have to be very secret. To think that my name is written on a government blacklist is enough to make me lose hope, but my name is also written in the Lamb's Book of Life. I don't know what the future will hold. Perhaps I will lose my job or even languish in jail, but I believe God is in control of everything. Whatever I have to face is all according to His perfect will.[22]

## 2007

In the past few years I have spread the gospel in various provinces. Now, my family and I are serving in a prosperous city, but without any systematic theological training I am learning as I minister. Many entrepreneurs here welcome church members to spread the gospel among their staff, but because of my limited knowledge I don't know how to share the gospel with the better-educated workers. Please pray for me.[23]

## 2008

Conservative estimates put the number of migrant workers in Wenzhou at two million. Just those living in the area near our church number 35,000. The workers are faced with many complex issues, such as the common occurrences of pregnancy out of wedlock and rampant divorce. We therefore established marriage counseling to help them, and we take the opportunity to share the gospel with those who attend. We very much need books on marriage counseling.[24]

## 2009

A church here in Zhejiang has spent more than nine million Yuan (approximately US$1.3 million) on building a church (including the land and construction fees), but they only have a congregation of 300 to 400 people, and there are few regular worshippers on Sundays. Most members are from farming areas and cannot afford to give large offerings. The construction costs were paid for by two brothers who run businesses, on top of a four million Yuan loan. The church's obligation to pay back the loan has restricted the development of their ministries.[25]

# 2010s

―――・◦・―――

## A megachurch fixation

The 2010s got underway with the struggle between the Communist authorities and the Church in Zhejiang taking a breather, before the conflict reached fever pitch later in the decade.

Throughout the province the apparent infatuation of many church leaders with large church buildings continued, despite the brutal campaign that had reduced more than 1,000 church buildings to rubble just a few years earlier.

As more Christians in the major cities of Zhejiang became financially richer due to China's booming economy, church leaders found the offerings they received enabled them to construct massive worship halls. A number of Western-style megachurches emerged throughout the province, among both Three-Self churches and the registered house church congregations of Wenzhou.

Many Zhejiang Christians now had the means to travel overseas, and were often impressed by the giant church buildings they saw in the United States and elsewhere. "Bigger is better" appeared to be the motto of the day, and church leaders in Zhejiang now had the money to fulfill their ambitions.

In Hangzhou, the Chongyi Three-Self Church had a humble beginning, when the China Inland Mission purchased a plot of land and built a small worship hall in 1901. A hundred years later, in 2003, after collecting 40 million Yuan ($6.7 million) from its members, the Chongyi Church began constructing a massive new edifice, which was finally

*The Chongyi Three-Self Church in Hangzhou, which seats up to 14,000 people*

Pieter Kwant

completed in May 2005. The enormous building regularly hosted a crowd of 5,500 believers in the main auditorium, but on special occasions much larger gatherings were held. In 2008 the American evangelist Franklin Graham addressed

12,000 people there, while in 2014 Luis Palau spoke to an estimated 14,000.

Similar huge buildings surfaced in Wenzhou and other parts of Zhejiang, leaving some visitors thankful to God at the presence of these overt religious symbols in places the Communist authorities had once vowed would be "religion-free zones." Other Christians, however, felt very uncomfortable with this new emphasis on buildings. They failed to see the wisdom in spending vast sums of money on facilities dedicated to worshipping a God who declared that He "does not live in temples built by human hands" (Acts 17.24).

The contrast between the megachurches of urban Zhejiang and the humble house church gatherings that continued to be the backbone of Christianity in the province was stark. China expert Brent Fulton pointed out some of the dangers of the "megachurch" mentality in China, writing:

> With the highest Christian population of any Chinese city, Wenzhou has become famous for its many towering structures, some of which, resembling European-style cathedrals, are quite striking. In the words of one observer . . . "Competition to build churches had almost become the order of the day. As soon as a new church was built, it was torn down and rebuilt again! Before the new building was even filled with people, they began to build an even bigger and more luxurious one . . . Many believers mistakenly think that tithing to support building a church building is the same as building a congregation. Since they believe this pleases God, they happily tithe to build a church building. Congregations often use church building projects as a means of uniting believers."[1]

As the years went by, indications emerged that many church leaders in Zhejiang were growing tired of the fixation with large buildings. They saw that the structures didn't bring the spiritual life and presence of the Holy Spirit they had once known in smaller gatherings, while the financial cost had become an unnecessary burden on their congregations. By 2013, some China observers had noted a shift in emphasis, with one remarking:

> On top of the financial concerns, a church building in China brings with it a whole new set of challenges, unlike anywhere else. There is always the possibility that the church will become regarded as a political threat, not to mention that a change in policy may lead to the meeting place being confiscated or even torn down at short (or no) notice . . .
>
> Several pastors in Wenzhou concede that some of the larger venues in their city have become white elephants. A congregation of a few hundred people is dwarfed by their newly constructed 1,000-seat premise . . . In another church, about 1,000 faithful regularly gather each week for worship in a venue that can accommodate more than 3,500. It is no longer a given that a new church building is a positive testimony. It can be something that is laughed at by officials and the local community.[2]

## *An unexpected twist*

At various times throughout the 2010s, the authorities in Zhejiang launched attacks against church buildings and believers. The pressure had reached boiling point by the middle of the decade, when a new and sustained campaign to remove crosses and to demolish church buildings commenced in earnest.

Often the government's justification for destroying church buildings was that the correct permits had not been obtained, or that obscure building code violations had been committed. While this is undoubtedly true in some cases, most of the time the crackdowns were launched without any legal basis, revealing that the real motive was to stop the spread of Christianity rather than to enforce local laws and regulations.

*Worshippers at the Three-Self church in Leqing, Zhejiang*
RCMI

A sign of what was to come took place in August 2010, when a large group of 200 Public Security officers burst into a prayer center known as "Prayer Mountain." The facility, owned by the Taishan Christian House Church in Taizhou City, was a place where believers could stay for times of concentrated intercession. On the morning of August 30, however, several elderly Christians were disturbed and pushed aside by the officers, who then proceeded to dismantle the building until it was a pile of rubble.[3]

By 2014, the Christian landscape in Zhejiang had experienced a shocking twist, with many registered Three-Self churches also finding themselves in the government's crosshairs. One of the highest-profile cases was the demolition of the large Sanjiang Three-Self Church, which had become something of an architectural landmark on the Wenzhou skyline. More than 200 church members rushed to the church when news spread that a team of highly trained special forces had surrounded the property and were dismantling the building piece by piece.

Protests continued for weeks after the demolition, as angry believers demanded justice from the authorities. Their cries fell on deaf ears, and more than 200 Christian demonstrators were arrested and taken to prison.

At least ten more registered church buildings were destroyed in May 2014, as China's atheist leaders appeared determined to reverse the growth of Christianity in the province. Unlike in previous years, they seemed unconcerned about the negative worldwide publicity their actions attracted. In July 2014, the large Salvation Church in Pingyang County near Wenzhou was the latest church targeted for demolition, but hundreds of members barricaded themselves inside the building and fought the riot police.

In an era of immediate global communications, the clash between the helmeted riot police and believers was captured on video and broadcast around the world, including by CNN.[4] The footage showed police savagely beating the protestors and dragging them away, as hundreds of people surged against the officers, trying to stop them from entering the building.

## *The anti-cross campaign*

From 2014 onwards, the pressure against Christians in Wenzhou appeared to focus more on removing the red crosses adorning churches in the city, and less on demolishing entire buildings. One China expert offered this explanation:

> The attack on the visible image of the cross and, by extension, upon the church's public presence, is rooted in the Party's deeper concern about any group in society that may pose a threat to its power. Christianity has attracted younger, well-educated

*The government removed thousands of crosses from churches in Zhejiang during a sustained campaign from 2014 to 2017*
VOM

followers in recent decades, who have developed not only a strong personal loyalty to the faith but also relational ties to Christians overseas . . .

If the main purpose of the anti-cross campaign is to reduce the church's visibility, perhaps what is happening in Zhejiang is less about control and more about the "not-in-my-backyard" attitude of Party officials toward the Church's public presence. In any case, whether in public or private, the Church will continue to thrive.[5]

The anti-cross campaign in Zhejiang, which began in 2014 and was still in progress as this book went to print, expanded into other forms of persecution as it gathered momentum. The success in striking the visible symbols of Christianity in Zhejiang appeared to embolden officials in other provinces, with Christians being openly attacked in other parts of the country, including distant Inner Mongolia.

*The dramatic scene when the cross atop the Dongyang Church burst into flames as government officials removed it in June 2015*

China Aid

Officials in Wenzhou instituted a new policy called "Three Rectifications and One Demolition," which enabled them to move, close or destroy any church buildings if they determined it would enhance the neighborhood where they were located. In May 2016, the legally registered Zhuyang Three-Self Church was negotiating with the government about where the congregation could relocate to, when all of a sudden more than 100 officers razed the church building to the ground.

A touching scene ensued the following Sunday, when church members held a service among the ruins of their building. As they knelt amid the rubble to pray and worship, protest

*Believers in Zhuyang pray amid the rubble of their church in 2016*
China Aid

banners were erected which read: "We are strongly opposed to this brutal, violent forced demolition," "Illegal law enforcement is intolerable," and "The powerful are headstrong."[6]

## The sad case of Miao Zhitong

One of the most prominent house church leaders in the Wenzhou area during the past 30 years was Miao Zhitong (not to be confused with Miao Zizhong, the "Cedar of Lebanon" profiled in an earlier chapter).

Born in Zhejiang in 1942, Miao Zhitong lost both his parents before he reached his teens and was raised by relatives. Miao grew up in rebellion against God until the age of 23, when he repented of his sins and dedicated his life to the Lord's service. Respected journalist David Aikman visited Miao in Wenzhou in the early part of the twenty-first century and asked him to share his story. Aikman later wrote:

He sensed a call to be a full-time preacher in 1967, at the very height of the Cultural Revolution. It wasn't long before he began to receive what became annual arrests, beatings, and sessions of torture. At one point he was hung up by the arms before being pushed into a pool of sewage where it was hoped he would drown. He managed to wrestle himself away and plunged into a clean creek before the police grabbed him, took him to a Buddhist temple, tied him to a pillar, and then beat him with bamboo rods. Only the presence of a large group of Christians who showed up at the temple and bravely clamored for his release prevented Miao from being beaten to death on the spot.[7]

In the late 1970s Miao Zhitong was rearrested and paraded through the streets. He was forced to stand on the parapet of a bridge, where the officials intended to kill him by pushing him off the edge. Seeing what was about to occur, Miao began praying fervently. A violent storm suddenly blew in and the parade was cancelled.

Miao proved to be a popular pastor, and he succeeded in unifying various independent house churches in eastern Zhejiang during the 1980s. By the early 1990s he was respected as a man of God and a leading house church "uncle" in this part of China. The persecution Miao was called to endure never lessened over the years, and "between 1968 and 1988, he said, he had been arrested at least 20 times."[8]

It is always tempting to speak only of the good things Christians achieve in their lives, although the Bible never follows that principle but always presents the balanced truth. Sadly, despite decades of faithful service for the gospel, the last stage of Miao Zhitong's journey before his death in 2013 saw him involved in controversy and intense conflict with other Chinese church leaders.

According to the veteran American missionary Dennis Balcombe, who was a long-time acquaintance of Miao, a dramatic change came over the Wenzhou pastor after some overseas Charismatic leaders—including the late Peter Wagner, and David Wang of the mission organization Asian Outreach—visited China in 2008 and anointed Miao Zhitong the "First Apostle of China" since the Communist Revolution.[9]

This ordination—done without the consultation or agreement of other Chinese church leaders—appeared to have an immediate negative effect on Miao's character. He seemed to revel in his newfound status, and pride flooded his heart. Whereas generations of believers knew Miao as a humble and selfless leader who was willing to endure great hardship for the gospel, conflict quickly developed between him and other church leaders. Miao also began to strongly attack other Chinese pastors whom he didn't consider worthy of the attention they were receiving.

Miao traveled overseas to speak at meetings, but the recordings made their way back into China, causing great alarm and fury among many house church pastors, including some of Miao's own co-workers. At the time, Miao was the leader of a number of house churches in the Rui'an City area of Zhejiang, with a total membership of no more than 3,000 believers. In one meeting in Singapore that year, however, Miao and his companions ludicrously claimed he was the leader of 30 million believers in China. In other parts of the world the claim was made that he led ten million Christians.

The Christian leaders in Zhejiang who tried to engage with Miao were frustrated by his combative attitude. Many relationships were destroyed, and Miao found himself marginalized and his influence confined to the Wenzhou area, whereas in previous times he had traveled widely throughout China. Balcombe lamented:

> Serious division arose between Miao and a large number of

people who at one time worked with him and highly respected him. Many of those leaders themselves had large followings and had sent out workers to many parts of China and pioneered many churches, but they now have no relationship with Miao.

Did Peter Wagner and the other "apostles" discern that Miao had serious conflict with a large number of leaders in China and overseas? How can someone be an "apostle" over people whom he attacks and goes to no limits to discredit?

I still respect Miao for his years of faithful service and sufferings for Christ; however, nobody has been able to bring up these issues with him without being accused and attacked. Placing someone in apostolic authority who obviously doesn't have such authority or respect is certainly a recipe for more divisions in the future.[10]

Miao was ill in the months leading up to his death in 2013, and thankfully he humbled himself and reconciled with some of the offended church leaders. Overall, in the intervening years since Miao's passing, the controversies surrounding the final part of his life have largely been forgotten, and the lasting memory of Miao Zhitong is of a pioneer of the Chinese house church movement, whom God used to bless multitudes of believers.

## *A return to brutality*

Although the removal of crosses from church buildings was largely symbolic, in 2015 the authorities in Zhejiang intensified their persecution of Christians. Instead of focusing on bricks and mortar, they began targeting key church leaders, sending many of them to prison on extremely serious, trumped-up charges.

An ordained Three-Self pastor, Zhang Chongzhu, was arrested and placed under "residential surveillance in a designated location" in September 2015. These places are also known as "black jails," where inmates are tortured mercilessly in undisclosed facilities such as abandoned factories and old junkyards, or in highly fortified apartment buildings. After being formally expelled from the Three-Self Church, Zhang was charged with "stealing, spying, buying or illegally providing state secrets or intelligence to entities outside China."[11]

In early 2016 a married couple, Bao Guohua and Xing Wenxiang, who served as pastors of the Holy Love Christian Church, were sentenced to 14 and 12 years' imprisonment respectively after they opposed the removal of crosses.

Many other pastors were similarly charged and sentenced to prison throughout Zhejiang, and in 2017 the government installed video surveillance cameras in many Three-Self churches to monitor church activities and sermons, and to help officials identify church members with the latest facial-recognition software.

The most significant arrest was that of Joseph Gu Yuese, the pastor of the huge Chongyi megachurch in Hangzhou, where well-known Western evangelists Franklin Graham and Luis Palau had preached to large crowds.

Gu's troubles began after he boldly criticized the government's cross removal campaign in 2014, even though at the time he was one of the main leaders of the Zhejiang TSPM and China Christian Council. In January 2016 he was forcibly removed from the ministry, and after being interrogated at a secret facility, he was charged with embezzling church funds. Gu was described as "the highest profile Christian official to be targeted since the Cultural Revolution," and his arrest caused great concern: "It will shake the spirit of the government-sanctioned church leaders and the congregations throughout China. All these factors will have a ripple effect."[12]

## The kingdom marches on

Although the many high-profile arrests and persecutions grabbed the headlines in Zhejiang throughout this difficult period, the kingdom of God continued to quietly advance, with hundreds of thousands of hungry souls entering through the Door of Salvation. Two letters received from Christians in Zhejiang helped remind people in other parts of the world of the daily struggles faced by millions of believers throughout the province. The first letter was from a young Christian woman recently diagnosed with cancer:

I have breast cancer. In the face of my illness I'm terribly frightened. I am just 36 years old. Despite being a believer, I'm not ready to die. I am still young and have not yet really lived the Christian life. I also want to influence others for Christ. I am afraid of death. My son is just six and needs so much of my care. My husband is a good man, making it hard for me to let go. I must be strong and not fall into bitterness as a result of the painful treatment.[13]

In a province where many urban churches had chased after expensive buildings and were now counting the cost in both financial and spiritual terms, it was easy to forget the numerous rural districts throughout Zhejiang where millions of Christians live, eking out a living from the land while demonstrating simple faith in Jesus. Asia Harvest received the following letter of appreciation after delivering a load of Bibles to a rural house church in the province:

*A Three-Self church in Wenzhou in 2018. The sign says: "The Party and government orders that Communist Party members, government officials, children, students and military people are forbidden to attend any church activities"*

Words cannot express the gratitude that our family feels for the Bibles you provided to us. We treasure them and read God's Word every day. Learning the words of our Lord makes our hearts overflow with joy. For so many years we longed to know the truth, and now we understand more every day and our faith has become stronger. God bless you for your sacrificial giving so that we can know the truth![14]

## *A socialist Bible*

The pressure against the Church was ramped up in 2017, as local authorities gradually implemented President Xi Jinping's

*A pure faith. Worshippers at Ningbo, Zhejiang*
RCMI

draconian campaign to eradicate what he calls "illegal religion" in China. Sunday schools were ordered to close throughout Zhejiang, and many Christian day-care centers had their business licenses revoked.[15]

The government appeared to be particularly determined to stop missionaries going out from Zhejiang to unreached nations. In January 2018, 14 Wenzhou believers who were involved in their church's Middle East mission program suddenly went missing in China. For weeks no news was received about their whereabouts, until they re-emerged in mid-February. The details of what had taken place and the conditions of their release were not clear.[16]

In some places, Christian families were visited and told to pull down Christian posters and banners from their home and replace them with pictures of Mao Zedong or Xi Jinping. Elderly believers who relied on their government pension to survive were told to abandon their faith and embrace socialism. Some were even ordered to stop thanking God for their daily provisions, but to give thanks to the Communist Party instead and to recognize it as their source of blessing.

In late 2018, news emerged of the government's strategy to implement a five-year plan to revise parts of the Bible in order to "promote the Sinicization of Christianity." The *Christian Post* reported:

> The plan, finalized at a meeting this March, proposes "culti-vating and implementing the socialist core values" and will be supervised by the national Religious Affairs Bureau. To "sinicize" (bring under Chinese control) Christianity, the gov-ernment plans to "retranslate" the Old Testament and provide new commentary to the New Testament . . .
>
> A retranslation would be a summary of the Old Testament with some Buddhist scripture and Confucian teachings, and new commentary for the New Testament . . .
>
> The five-year plan advocates "incorporating Chinese ele-ments into church worship services, hymns and songs, clergy attire, and the architectural style of church buildings." Church leaders must pledge their loyalty to the Communist Party. The first criteria they have to pass is whether they can publicly pledge they will uphold the Party's words and path.[17]

Meanwhile, Zhejiang appeared to be at the center of President Xi's campaign to control Christianity. According to a report, in October 2018:

> More than 300 Christian children in two high schools in Zhejiang were asked to fill out a form stating that they did not follow a religion . . .
>
> Schools in China are government-controlled and financed and therefore Communist in ideology, and Christian children have sometimes faced "shaming" incidents, but the extent of such shaming was to prevent them from joining the Communist

Youth League, thereby denying them any of the perks that come with a progression to Communist Party membership later in life . . .

In the first school, which has around 200 Christian students, the teacher demanded they rewrite the questionnaire, stating that they had "no religion." But when filling out the next questionnaire, half of the children maintained that they were Christians. Following further warnings, in the end all but one child complied.

In the other school, which has around 100 children, it was the class prefect who forced the Christians to resubmit their papers, stating that they had no religion . . .

Children who do not comply are reportedly denied access to opportunities at school, such as being elected as a class representative for special events. They could also potentially face the danger of not receiving a leaving certificate from their school and therefore not be able to attend university. Such incidents are also recorded in the child's personal file which is held by local government departments, and the information can hamper their future employment opportunities.[18]

The fanatical crackdown on the Church in China continued to intensify. At the time of this book going to print, many Zhejiang church leaders were under grave pressure, with some saying they were experiencing the most brutal attack on the faith since the darkest days of the Cultural Revolution.

By early 2019, many Christians in Zhejiang had gone into survival mode. In a return to the atmosphere of life in the 1960s, large congregations broke down into small groups of four or five believers, who discreetly gathered together for Bible study and prayer. Many house church pastors went into hiding, turning off their phones and other electronic devices because of the government's invasive ability to track its citizens.

# The future of the Church in Zhejiang

As we reach the end of our look at the wonderful things God has done in Zhejiang Province, one thing is clear: despite decades of battering and persecution, the Lord Jesus Christ has raised up a vibrant body from among Zhejiang's population of more than 60 million people.

The early Evangelical missionaries in the nineteenth century overcame overwhelming obstacles to plant the seed of the gospel in the province. Instead of God sending the strong to establish His kingdom in Zhejiang, He sent the one-legged George Stott who was pelted with stones by hostile locals. Many other faithful missionaries served in the coastal province, including James Meadows, who spent more than half a century in Zhejiang, and the intrepid Hudson Taylor, who first had to overcome deep hostility from the mission community to marry the woman God had set apart to be his wife.

The 1920s and 1930s witnessed an outbreak of revival in Zhejiang, with Chinese evangelists at the forefront. "China's greatest preacher" John Sung visited several times, and Dora Yu Cidu was used greatly by the Holy Spirit to bring spiritual life and vitality to Christians when they needed a boost due to the distressed conditions of the time.

As the Church gradually passed from foreign to Chinese control, it matured and strengthened into a powerful remnant that was able to withstand decades of hardship. The early missionaries had steadfastly refused to finance the Chinese in any gospel work that they themselves should fund, and their tenacious approach paid off. When all foreigners were expelled from China, the Church in Zhejiang continued preaching the gospel with few interruptions, whereas in other provinces the Church struggled to survive when the foreign support was taken away.

Zhejiang's Christians saw the dark storm clouds gathering on the horizon as the Communists swept to power in the 1940s, so they strengthened one another and braced themselves for difficult times ahead. The severe hardship arrived in the 1950s. Forty-nine church leaders from the city of Wenzhou were sent to prison labor camps. Only one man, Miao Zizhong, returned home alive. His remarkable testimony earned him the nickname "the Cedar of Lebanon" from other believers.

In the 1960s the government strongly attacked the Christians in Zhejiang, but the more the Church was persecuted, the stronger it seemed to become. At one stage, infuriated by the continuing expansion of Christianity, the authorities launched a campaign to make Wenzhou a "religion-free zone," but their attempts proved futile. Instead, the city emerged as an engine room for Christianity, and earned the nickname "the Jerusalem of China."

When China awoke from decades of brutal persecution in the 1980s, Christians around the world were amazed to discover that not only had Christianity survived in Zhejiang, but in many places it had grown and prospered! Miracles occurred throughout the province as a massive revival gained momentum, transforming the lives of millions of people from all walks of life.

Today, Zhejiang holds the honor of being the province of China with the highest percentage of Christians. It also appears to be unique in China in that the majority of Christians are men. In many other provinces the churches are dominated by female believers.

As the table in the back of this book reveals, there are more than ten million Evangelical Christians throughout Zhejiang

Province today, with approximately 4.2 million believers attending the registered Three-Self churches, and 6.2 million who are part of house church networks found throughout every part of the province.

An additional 2.8 million Catholics are estimated to reside in Zhejiang today, most of whom are part of independent house churches. In total, 13.3 million people in Zhejiang are estimated to now profess faith in Jesus Christ, which amounts to more than one fifth (21.2 percent) of the entire population of the province. Zhejiang sits comfortably ahead of the province in second place, Henan, where 15.7 percent of the population are professing Christians.

There is much to praise God for as we consider the marvelous things He has done in Zhejiang! At the same time, developments in the last 20 years give cause for concern. As the Chinese economy boomed, the savvy Christian business people of cities like Wenzhou and Hangzhou took advantage of the new freedoms, and the churches in those cities became very wealthy.

To start with, church leaders used the newfound wealth to spread the gospel throughout China and even overseas. In more recent times, however, the construction of elaborate church buildings has become a wasteful infatuation for many church leaders. They rushed headlong into the same error as the Church in other parts of the world, believing that massive edifices are pleasing to God and indicative of His blessing. Hundreds of millions of dollars have been spent on the construction of church buildings in Zhejiang, many of which have subsequently been demolished or closed by the government.

In recent years the world's media has reported the cutting down of crosses from thousands of church buildings in Wenzhou, but the campaign has been of little consequence to the real work of the gospel in Zhejiang. At the time of this book going to print, the churches in the province were a diverse group, ranging from megachurches in the wealthy coastal cities, to poor rural fellowships in inland areas where impoverished members struggle to eke out a living.

Although Zhejiang today contains many believers who are wrapped up in the empty "prosperity gospel," millions of other Christians daily present their lives as living sacrifices to the Lord Jesus Christ. They continue to be persecuted for their faith, and they simply love the Lord and long for His Name to be glorified among people everywhere.

Starting in 2016, the situation began to change dramatically for believers in Zhejiang as the government signaled its intention to control, and ultimately destroy, grass-roots Christianity. Thousands of churches throughout the province were forced to close their doors, and numerous house church pastors were instructed to register with the Three-Self Church or face dire consequences. Sunday schools were made illegal, and wide-ranging pressure was placed on Christians to renounce their faith and embrace atheistic Communist ideology.

The impending implementation of China's "social credit" system in 2020, which has the potential to take away the ability of Christians to travel, work, and ultimately to buy and sell, threatens to pose the greatest challenge for the faith in Zhejiang—greater even than the excesses of the Cultural Revolution or the aggressive persecutions against the Church in recent years.

For nearly 200 years the Evangelical enterprise in Zhejiang has been characterized by deep devotion to Christ, simple faith and fervent preaching of the gospel. How the Church in Zhejiang handles the present crisis will determine the future for Christianity in the province. Either it will continue to enjoy a bright era, or it will compromise and lose the sharp spiritual edge that has characterized it throughout history, when generations of believers emptied their lives before God, gaining a vibrant and unbreakable faith that catapulted the province into its current position: having the highest concentration of Christians in China today.

# *Appendix*

## Table 2 Evangelical Christians in Zhejiang (1843–2020)

(Both Three-Self and house churches)

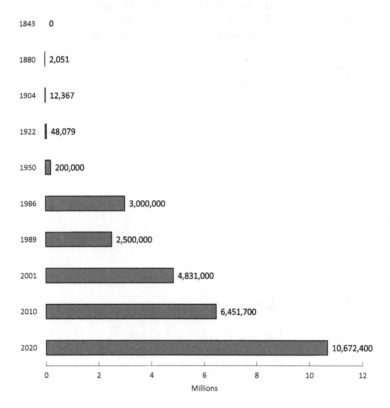

# Appendix

*Sources:*

| | |
|---|---|
| 0 | (1843) |
| 2,051 | (1880 – *Chinese Recorder*, July 1880) |
| 12,367 | (1904 – *China's Millions*, November 1905) |
| 48,079 | (1922 – Stauffer, *The Christian Occupation of China*) |
| 200,000 | (1950 – *China Study Journal*, December 1992) |
| 700,000 | (1984 – in 1,200 churches, *Bridge*, March–April 1984)* |
| 3,000,000 | (1986 – *Pray for China*, January–February 1986) |
| 2,500,000 | (1989 – Lambert, *The Resurrection of the Chinese Church*) |
| 1,200,000 | (1994 – Amity News Service, April 1994)* |
| 4,831,000 | (2001 – Johnstone and Mandryk, *Operation World*) |
| 1,834,000 | (2004 – Amity News Service, November–December 2004)* |
| 6,451,700 | (2010 – Mandryk, *Operation World*) |
| 10,672,400 | (2020 – Hattaway, The China Chronicles) |

* These sources may only refer to registered church estimates. Three-Self figures typically only count adult baptized members.

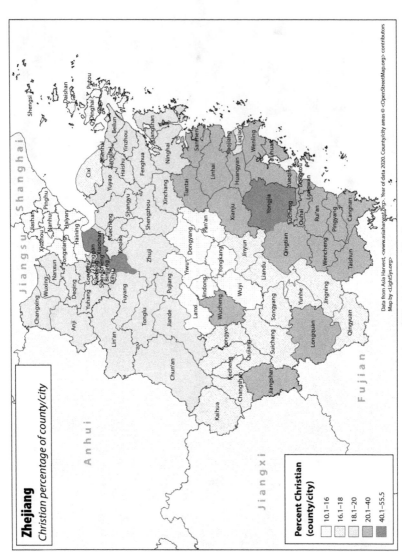

*Map of Christians in Zhejiang*

Data from Asia Harvest, <www.asiaharvest.org>. Year of data 2020. County/city areas © <OpenStreetMap.org> contributors. Map by <Lightsys.org>

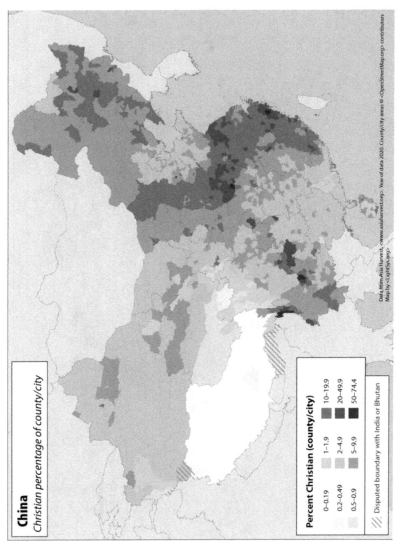

**China**
*Christian percentage of county/city*

**Percent Christian (county/city)**

- 0–0.19
- 0.2–0.49
- 0.5–0.9
- 1–1.9
- 2–4.9
- 5–9.9
- 10–19.9
- 20–49.9
- 50–74.4

/// Disputed boundary with India or Bhutan

Data from Asia Harvest, <www.asiaharvest.org>. Year of data 2020. County/city areas © <OpenStreetMap.org> contributors. Map by <LightSys.org>

*Map of China's Christians*

# A survey of Christians in China

For centuries, people have been curious to know how many Christians live in China. When Marco Polo made his famous journey to the Orient 750 years ago, he revealed the existence of Nestorian churches and monasteries in various places, to the fascination of people back in Europe.

Since I started traveling to China in the 1980s, I have found that Christians around the world are still eager to know how many believers there are in China. Many people are aware that God has done a remarkable work in the world's most populated country, but little research has been done to put a figure on this phenomenon. In recent decades, wildly divergent estimates have been published, ranging from 20 million to 230 million Christians in China.

## Methodology

In Table 3, I provide estimates of the number of Christians in Zhejiang. Full tables of the other provinces of China can be found at the Asia Harvest website (see the "The Church in China" link under the Resources tab at <www.asiaharvest.org>). My survey provides figures for Christians of every creed, arranged in four main categories: the Three-Self Patriotic Movement; the Evangelical house churches; the Catholic Patriotic Association; and the Catholic house churches. I have supplied statistics for all 2,370 cities and counties within every province, municipality and autonomous region of China.

The information was gathered from a wide variety of sources. More than 2,000 published sources have been noted in the tables published online, including a multitude of books, journals, magazine articles and reports that I spent years meticulously accumulating. I have also conducted hundreds of hours of interviews with key house church leaders responsible for their church networks throughout China.

Before entering data into the tables, I began with this assumption: that in any given place in China there are no Christians at all, until I have a figure from a documented source or can make an intelligent estimate based on information gathered from Chinese Christian leaders. In other words, I wanted to put aside all preconceptions and expectations, input all the information I had, and see what the totals came to.

## A note about security

None of the information provided in these tables is new to the Chinese government. Beijing has already thoroughly researched the spread of Christianity throughout the country, as shown by high-ranking official Ye Xiaowen's 2006 announcement that there were then 130 million Christians in China. In December 2009, the national newspaper *China Daily* interviewed scholar Liu Peng who had spent years researching religion for the Chinese Academy of Social Sciences. Liu claimed the "house churches have at least 50 million followers nationwide." His figure at the time was consistent with my research.

After consulting various house church leaders in China, I was able to confirm that all of them were content that this information should be published, as long as the surveys focus on statistics and avoid specific information such as the names and locations of Christian leaders.

## The Chinese Church in perspective

All discussion of how many Christians there are in China today should be tempered by the realization that more than 90 percent of the population faces a Christless eternity. Hundreds of millions of individuals have yet to hear the gospel. Church leaders in China have told me how ashamed and burdened they feel that so many of their countrymen and women do not yet know Jesus Christ. This burden motivates them to do whatever it takes to preach the gospel among every ethnic group and in every city, town and village—to every individual—in China, and to do whatever necessary to see Christ exalted throughout the land.

May we humbly give thanks to the living God for the great things He has done in China. We are privileged to live in a remarkable time in human history, like the days prophesied by the prophet Habakkuk:

> Look at the nations and watch—and be utterly amazed. For I am going to do something in your days that you would not believe, even if you were told.
>
> (Habakkuk 1.5)

# Table 3 Christians in Zhejiang

| Location | | POPULATION | | | | | CHRISTIANS | | | | | | Total Christians | |
|---|---|---|---|---|---|---|---|---|---|---|---|---|---|---|
| | | | | | | | Evangelicals | | | Catholics | | | | |
| Zhejiang 浙江 | | Census 2000 | Census 2010 | Growth | Growth (percent) | Estimate 2020 | TSPM | House church | TOTAL Evangelicals | CPA | House church | TOTAL Catholics | TOTAL | Percent of 2020 population |
| **Hangzhou Prefecture** | 杭州市 | | | | | | | | | | | | | |
| Binjiang District | 滨江区 | 115,887 | 319,027 | 203,140 | 175.29 | 522,167 | 31,330 | 43,862 | 75,192 | 8,877 | 17,754 | 26,631 | 101,823 | 19.50 |
| Chun'an County | 淳安县 | 382,347 | 336,843 | -45,504 | -11.90 | 291,339 | 17,480 | 24,472 | 41,953 | 4,953 | 9,906 | 14,858 | 56,811 | 19.50 |
| Fuyang District | 富阳区 | 628,633 | 717,694 | 89,061 | 14.17 | 806,755 | 48,405 | 67,767 | 116,173 | 13,715 | 27,430 | 41,145 | 157,317 | 19.50 |
| Gongshu District | 拱墅区 | 429,292 | 551,874 | 122,582 | 28.55 | 674,456 | 40,467 | 56,654 | 97,122 | 11,466 | 22,932 | 34,397 | 131,519 | 19.50 |
| Jiande City | 建德市 | 473,062 | 430,750 | -42,312 | -8.94 | 388,438 | 23,306 | 32,629 | 55,935 | 6,603 | 13,207 | 19,810 | 75,745 | 19.50 |
| Jiangan District | 江干区 | 565,360 | 998,783 | 433,423 | 76.66 | 1,432,206 | 85,932 | 120,305 | 206,238 | 24,348 | 48,695 | 73,043 | 279,280 | 19.50 |
| Lin'an District | 临安区 | 514,238 | 566,665 | 52,427 | 10.20 | 619,092 | 37,146 | 52,004 | 89,149 | 10,525 | 21,049 | 31,574 | 120,723 | 19.50 |
| Shangcheng District | 上城区 | 335,050 | 344,594 | 9,544 | 2.85 | 354,138 | 21,248 | 29,748 | 50,996 | 6,020 | 12,041 | 18,061 | 69,057 | 19.50 |
| Tonglu County | 桐庐县 | 378,060 | 406,450 | 28,390 | 7.51 | 434,840 | 26,090 | 36,527 | 62,617 | 7,392 | 14,785 | 22,177 | 84,794 | 19.50 |
| Xiacheng District | 下城区 | 412,406 | 526,096 | 113,690 | 27.57 | 639,786 | 38,387 | 53,742 | 92,129 | 10,876 | 21,753 | 32,629 | 124,758 | 19.50 |
| Xiaoshan District | 萧山区 | 1,233,348 | 1,511,290 | 277,942 | 22.54 | 1,789,232 | 146,001 | 586,331 | 732,333 | 30,417 | 60,834 | 91,251 | 823,583 | 46.03 |
| Xihu District | 西湖区 | 593,324 | 820,017 | 226,693 | 38.21 | 1,046,710 | 62,803 | 87,924 | 150,726 | 17,794 | 35,588 | 53,382 | 204,108 | 19.50 |
| Yuhang District | 余杭区 | 817,715 | 1,170,290 | 352,575 | 43.12 | 1,522,865 | 91,372 | 127,921 | 219,293 | 25,889 | 51,777 | 77,666 | 296,959 | 19.50 |
| | | 6,878,722 | 8,700,373 | 1,821,651 | 26.48 | 10,522,024 | 669,969 | 1,319,886 | 1,989,855 | 178,874 | 357,749 | 536,623 | 2,526,478 | 24.01 |
| **Huzhou Prefecture** | 湖州市 | | | | | | | | | | | | | |
| Anji County | 安吉县 | 432,139 | 466,552 | 34,413 | 7.96 | 500,965 | 30,058 | 42,081 | 72,139 | 8,516 | 17,033 | 25,549 | 97,688 | 19.50 |
| Changxing County | 长兴县 | 611,518 | 641,982 | 30,464 | 4.98 | 672,446 | 40,347 | 56,485 | 96,832 | 11,432 | 22,863 | 34,295 | 131,127 | 19.50 |
| Deqing County | 德清县 | 436,524 | 491,789 | 55,265 | 12.66 | 547,054 | 32,823 | 45,953 | 78,776 | 9,300 | 18,600 | 27,900 | 106,676 | 19.50 |
| Nanxun District | 南浔区 | 536,054 | 536,054 | 0 | 0.00 | 536,054 | 32,163 | 45,029 | 77,192 | 9,113 | 18,226 | 27,339 | 104,531 | 19.50 |
| Wuxing District | 吴兴区 | 757,165 | 757,165 | 0 | 0.00 | 757,165 | 45,430 | 63,602 | 109,032 | 12,872 | 25,744 | 38,615 | 147,647 | 19.50 |
| | | 2,625,595 | 2,893,542 | 120,142 | 4.58 | 3,013,684 | 180,821 | 253,149 | 433,970 | 51,233 | 102,465 | 153,698 | 587,668 | 19.50 |
| **Jiaxing Prefecture** | 嘉兴市 | | | | | | | | | | | | | |
| Haining City | 海宁市 | 666,080 | 806,966 | 140,886 | 21.15 | 947,852 | 47,393 | 66,350 | 113,742 | 9,479 | 18,957 | 28,436 | 142,178 | 15.00 |
| Haiyan County | 海盐县 | 387,723 | 430,940 | 43,217 | 11.15 | 474,157 | 23,708 | 33,191 | 56,899 | 4,742 | 9,483 | 14,225 | 71,124 | 15.00 |
| Jiashan County | 嘉善县 | 425,972 | 574,187 | 148,215 | 34.79 | 722,402 | 36,120 | 50,568 | 86,688 | 5,779 | 11,558 | 17,338 | 104,026 | 14.40 |
| Nanhu District | 南湖区 | 500,298 | 612,663 | 112,365 | 22.46 | 725,028 | 36,251 | 50,752 | 87,003 | 7,250 | 14,501 | 21,751 | 108,754 | 15.00 |
| Pinghu City | 平湖市 | 507,899 | 671,834 | 163,935 | 32.28 | 835,769 | 41,788 | 58,504 | 100,292 | 8,358 | 16,715 | 25,073 | 125,365 | 15.00 |
| Tongxiang City | 桐乡市 | 713,399 | 815,848 | 102,449 | 14.36 | 918,297 | 45,915 | 64,281 | 110,196 | 9,183 | 18,366 | 27,549 | 137,745 | 15.00 |
| Xiuzhou District | 秀洲区 | 381,625 | 589,219 | 207,594 | 54.40 | 796,813 | 39,841 | 55,777 | 95,618 | 7,968 | 15,936 | 23,904 | 119,522 | 15.00 |
| | | 3,582,996 | 4,501,657 | 918,661 | 25.64 | 5,420,318 | 271,016 | 379,422 | 650,438 | 52,758 | 105,517 | 158,275 | 808,713 | 14.92 |
| **Jinhua Prefecture** | 金华市 | | | | | | | | | | | | | |
| Dongyang City | 东阳市 | 753,094 | 804,398 | 51,304 | 6.81 | 855,702 | 51,342 | 71,879 | 123,221 | 4,279 | 8,557 | 12,836 | 136,057 | 15.90 |
| Jindong District | 金东区 | 475,800 | 315,583 | -160,217 | -33.67 | 155,366 | 9,322 | 13,051 | 22,373 | 777 | 1,554 | 2,330 | 24,703 | 15.90 |
| Lanxi City | 兰溪市 | 607,196 | 560,514 | -46,682 | -7.69 | 513,832 | 30,830 | 43,162 | 73,992 | 2,569 | 5,138 | 7,707 | 81,699 | 15.90 |
| Pan'an County | 磐安县 | 175,834 | 174,665 | -1,169 | -0.66 | 173,496 | 10,410 | 14,574 | 24,983 | 867 | 1,735 | 2,602 | 27,586 | 15.90 |
| Pujiang County | 浦江县 | 364,138 | 437,346 | 73,208 | 20.10 | 510,554 | 40,130 | 56,181 | 96,311 | 511 | 1,021 | 1,532 | 97,843 | 19.16 |
| Wucheng District | 婺城区 | 424,859 | 761,662 | 336,803 | 79.27 | 1,098,465 | 86,339 | 120,875 | 207,214 | 5,492 | 10,985 | 16,477 | 223,691 | 20.36 |
| Wuyi County | 武义县 | 301,223 | 349,899 | 48,676 | 16.16 | 398,575 | 23,915 | 33,480 | 57,395 | 1,993 | 3,986 | 5,979 | 63,373 | 15.90 |
| Yiwu City | 义乌市 | 912,670 | 1,234,015 | 321,345 | 35.21 | 1,555,360 | 62,214 | 87,100 | 149,315 | 7,777 | 15,553 | 23,330 | 172,645 | 11.10 |
| Yongkang City | 永康市 | 557,067 | 723,490 | 166,423 | 29.87 | 889,913 | 32,660 | 45,724 | 78,384 | 4,450 | 8,899 | 13,349 | 91,732 | 10.31 |
| | | 4,571,881 | 5,361,572 | 789,691 | 17.27 | 6,151,263 | 347,161 | 486,026 | 833,187 | 28,714 | 57,428 | 86,142 | 919,330 | 14.95 |

**Zhejiang 浙江**

| | POPULATION | | | | | CHRISTIANS | | | | | | | |
|---|---|---|---|---|---|---|---|---|---|---|---|---|---|
| | | | | | | Evangelicals | | | Catholics | | | Total Christians | |
| Location | Census 2000 | Census 2010 | Growth | Growth (percent) | Estimate 2020 | TSPM | House church | TOTAL Evangelicals | CPA | House church | TOTAL Catholics | TOTAL | Percent of 2020 population |
| **Lishui Prefecture 丽水市** | | | | | | | | | | | | | |
| Jingning County 景宁畲族自治县 | 153,011 | 107,106 | -45,905 | -30.00 | 61,201 | 3,060 | 4,284 | 7,344 | 1,040 | 2,081 | 3,121 | 10,465 | 17.10 |
| Jinyun County 缙云县 | 362,252 | 358,917 | -3,335 | -0.92 | 355,582 | 17,779 | 24,891 | 42,670 | 6,045 | 12,090 | 18,135 | 60,805 | 17.10 |
| Liandu District 莲都区 | 348,241 | 451,418 | 103,177 | 29.63 | 554,595 | 27,730 | 38,822 | 66,551 | 9,428 | 18,856 | 28,284 | 94,836 | 17.10 |
| Longquan City 龙泉市 | 250,398 | 234,626 | -15,772 | -6.30 | 218,854 | 17,508 | 24,512 | 42,020 | 3,721 | 7,441 | 11,162 | 53,182 | 24.30 |
| Qingtian County 青田县 | 361,062 | 336,542 | -24,520 | -6.79 | 312,022 | 37,443 | 52,420 | 89,862 | 10,609 | 5,304 | 15,913 | 105,775 | 33.90 |
| Qingyuan County 庆元县 | 179,449 | 141,541 | -37,908 | -21.12 | 103,633 | 5,182 | 7,254 | 12,436 | 1,762 | 3,524 | 5,285 | 17,721 | 17.10 |
| Songyang County 松阳县 | 197,340 | 185,051 | -12,289 | -6.23 | 172,762 | 8,638 | 12,093 | 20,731 | 2,937 | 5,874 | 8,811 | 29,542 | 17.10 |
| Suichang County 遂昌县 | 207,087 | 190,165 | -16,922 | -8.17 | 173,243 | 8,662 | 12,127 | 20,789 | 2,945 | 5,890 | 8,835 | 29,625 | 17.10 |
| Yunhe County 云和县 | 103,273 | 111,591 | 8,318 | 8.05 | 119,909 | 5,995 | 8,394 | 14,389 | 2,038 | 4,077 | 6,115 | 20,504 | 17.10 |
| | 2,162,113 | 2,116,957 | -45,156 | -2.09 | 2,071,801 | 131,997 | 184,796 | 316,793 | 35,221 | 70,441 | 105,662 | 422,455 | 20.39 |
| **Ningbo Prefecture 宁波市** | | | | | | | | | | | | | |
| Beilun District 北仑区 | 382,278 | 612,267 | 229,989 | 60.16 | 842,256 | 50,535 | 70,750 | 121,285 | 14,318 | 28,637 | 42,955 | 164,240 | 19.50 |
| Cixi City 慈溪市 | 1,214,537 | 1,462,383 | 247,846 | 20.41 | 1,710,229 | 102,614 | 143,659 | 246,273 | 14,537 | 29,074 | 43,611 | 289,884 | 16.95 |
| Fenghua District 奉化区 | 471,558 | 491,697 | 20,139 | 4.27 | 511,836 | 30,710 | 42,994 | 73,704 | 8,701 | 17,402 | 26,104 | 99,808 | 19.50 |
| Haishu District 海曙区 | 349,739 | 373,742 | 24,003 | 6.86 | 397,745 | 23,865 | 33,411 | 57,275 | 6,762 | 13,523 | 20,285 | 77,560 | 19.50 |
| Jiangbei District 江北区 | 271,223 | 361,242 | 90,019 | 33.19 | 451,261 | 27,076 | 37,906 | 64,982 | 7,671 | 15,343 | 23,014 | 87,996 | 19.50 |
| Jiangdong District 江东区 | 292,552 | 366,648 | 74,096 | 25.33 | 440,744 | 26,445 | 37,022 | 63,467 | 7,493 | 14,985 | 22,478 | 85,945 | 19.50 |
| Ninghai County 宁海县 | 518,186 | 646,074 | 127,888 | 24.68 | 773,962 | 46,438 | 65,013 | 111,451 | 13,157 | 26,315 | 39,472 | 150,923 | 19.50 |
| Xiangshan County 象山县 | 484,236 | 503,279 | 19,043 | 3.93 | 522,322 | 31,339 | 43,875 | 75,214 | 8,879 | 17,759 | 26,638 | 101,853 | 19.50 |
| Yinzhou District 鄞州区 | 854,627 | 1,359,198 | 504,571 | 59.04 | 1,863,769 | 111,826 | 156,557 | 268,383 | 31,684 | 63,368 | 95,052 | 363,435 | 19.50 |
| Yuyao City 余姚市 | 852,719 | 1,010,659 | 157,940 | 18.52 | 1,168,599 | 70,116 | 98,162 | 168,278 | 19,866 | 39,732 | 59,599 | 227,877 | 19.50 |
| Zhenhai District 镇海区 | 271,707 | 418,500 | 146,793 | 54.03 | 565,293 | 33,918 | 47,485 | 81,402 | 9,610 | 19,220 | 28,830 | 110,232 | 19.50 |
| | 5,963,362 | 7,605,689 | 1,642,327 | 27.54 | 9,248,016 | 554,881 | 776,833 | 1,331,714 | 142,679 | 285,359 | 428,038 | 1,759,752 | 19.03 |
| **Quzhou Prefecture 衢州市** | | | | | | | | | | | | | |
| Changshan County 常山县 | 265,467 | 241,368 | -24,099 | -9.08 | 217,269 | 10,972 | 15,361 | 26,333 | 3,694 | 7,387 | 11,081 | 37,414 | 17.22 |
| Jiangshan City 江山市 | 473,222 | 467,862 | -5,360 | -1.13 | 462,502 | 32,375 | 45,325 | 77,700 | 7,863 | 15,725 | 23,588 | 101,288 | 21.90 |
| Kaihua County 开化县 | 271,611 | 245,088 | -26,523 | -9.77 | 218,565 | 11,038 | 15,453 | 26,490 | 3,716 | 7,431 | 11,147 | 37,637 | 17.22 |
| Kecheng District 柯城区 | 286,271 | 464,527 | 178,256 | 62.27 | 642,783 | 32,461 | 45,445 | 77,905 | 10,927 | 21,855 | 32,782 | 110,687 | 17.22 |
| Longyou County 龙游县 | 368,157 | 362,380 | -5,777 | -1.57 | 356,603 | 18,008 | 25,212 | 43,220 | 6,062 | 12,125 | 18,187 | 61,407 | 17.22 |
| Qujiang District 衢江区 | 464,128 | 341,436 | -122,692 | -26.43 | 218,744 | 11,047 | 15,465 | 26,512 | 3,719 | 7,437 | 11,156 | 37,668 | 17.22 |
| | 2,128,856 | 2,122,661 | -6,195 | -0.29 | 2,116,466 | 115,900 | 162,260 | 278,161 | 35,980 | 71,960 | 107,940 | 386,101 | 18.24 |
| **Shaoxing Prefecture 绍兴市** | | | | | | | | | | | | | |
| Keqiao District 柯桥区 | 791,797 | 1,030,847 | 239,050 | 30.19 | 1,269,897 | 76,194 | 106,671 | 182,865 | 21,588 | 43,176 | 64,765 | 247,630 | 19.50 |
| Shangyu District 上虞区 | 722,523 | 779,412 | 56,889 | 7.87 | 836,301 | 50,178 | 70,249 | 120,427 | 14,217 | 28,434 | 42,651 | 163,079 | 19.50 |
| Shengzhou City 嵊州市 | 671,221 | 679,762 | 8,541 | 1.27 | 688,303 | 41,298 | 57,817 | 99,116 | 11,701 | 23,402 | 35,103 | 134,219 | 19.50 |
| Xinchang County 新昌县 | 414,907 | 380,444 | -34,463 | -8.31 | 345,981 | 20,759 | 29,062 | 49,821 | 5,882 | 11,763 | 17,645 | 67,466 | 19.50 |
| Yuecheng District 越城区 | 633,118 | 883,836 | 250,718 | 39.60 | 1,134,554 | 68,073 | 95,303 | 163,376 | 19,287 | 38,575 | 57,862 | 221,238 | 19.50 |
| Zhuji City 诸暨市 | 1,070,675 | 1,157,938 | 87,263 | 8.15 | 1,245,201 | 74,712 | 104,597 | 179,309 | 21,168 | 42,337 | 63,505 | 242,814 | 19.50 |
| | 4,304,241 | 4,912,239 | 607,998 | 14.13 | 5,520,237 | 331,214 | 463,700 | 794,914 | 93,844 | 187,688 | 281,532 | 1,076,446 | 19.50 |

| Zhejiang 浙江 | | POPULATION | | | | | CHRISTIANS | | | | | | Total Christians | |
| Location | | Census 2000 | Census 2010 | Growth | Growth (percent) | Estimate 2020 | Evangelicals | | | Catholics | | | | |
| | | | | | | | TSPM | House church | TOTAL Evangelicals | CPA | House church | TOTAL Catholics | TOTAL | Percent of 2020 population |
|---|---|---|---|---|---|---|---|---|---|---|---|---|---|---|
| **Taizhou Prefecture** 台州市 | | | | | | | | | | | | | | |
| Huangyan District 黄岩区 | | 564,120 | 632,123 | 68,003 | 12.05 | 700,126 | 45,508 | 63,711 | 109,220 | 11,902 | 23,804 | 35,706 | 144,926 | 20.70 |
| Jiaojiang District 椒江区 | | 462,846 | 653,765 | 190,919 | 41.25 | 844,684 | 54,904 | 76,866 | 131,771 | 14,360 | 28,719 | 43,079 | 174,850 | 20.70 |
| Linhai City 临海市 | | 948,618 | 1,028,813 | 80,195 | 8.45 | 1,109,008 | 72,086 | 100,920 | 173,005 | 18,853 | 37,706 | 56,559 | 229,565 | 20.70 |
| Luqiao District 路桥区 | | 464,997 | 616,622 | 151,625 | 32.61 | 768,247 | 42,254 | 59,155 | 101,409 | 13,060 | 26,120 | 39,181 | 140,589 | 18.30 |
| Sanmen County 三门县 | | 315,405 | 328,887 | 13,482 | 4.27 | 342,369 | 22,254 | 31,156 | 53,410 | 5,820 | 11,641 | 17,461 | 70,870 | 20.70 |
| Tiantai County 天台县 | | 407,270 | 382,812 | -24,458 | -6.01 | 358,354 | 23,293 | 32,610 | 55,903 | 6,092 | 12,184 | 18,276 | 74,179 | 20.70 |
| Wenling City 温岭市 | | 1,162,783 | 1,366,794 | 204,011 | 17.55 | 1,570,805 | 102,102 | 142,943 | 245,046 | 26,704 | 53,407 | 80,111 | 325,157 | 20.70 |
| Xianju County 仙居县 | | 367,585 | 342,676 | -24,909 | -6.78 | 317,767 | 20,655 | 28,917 | 49,572 | 5,402 | 10,804 | 16,206 | 65,778 | 20.70 |
| Yuhuan County 玉环县 | | 460,091 | 616,346 | 156,255 | 33.96 | 772,601 | 50,219 | 70,307 | 120,526 | 13,134 | 26,268 | 39,403 | 159,928 | 20.70 |
| | | 5,153,715 | 5,968,838 | 815,123 | 15.82 | 6,783,961 | 433,275 | 606,585 | 1,039,860 | 115,327 | 230,655 | 345,982 | 1,385,842 | 20.43 |
| **Wenzhou Prefecture** 温州市 | | | | | | | | | | | | | | |
| Cangnan County 苍南县 | | 1,167,589 | 1,184,643 | 17,054 | 1.46 | 1,201,697 | 122,573 | 171,602 | 294,175 | 20,429 | 56,840 | 77,269 | 371,445 | 30.91 |
| Dongtou District 洞头区 | | 96,435 | 87,683 | -8,752 | -9.08 | 78,931 | 8,051 | 11,271 | 19,322 | 1,342 | 2,684 | 4,025 | 23,348 | 29.58 |
| Longwan District 龙湾区 | | 204,935 | 749,303 | 544,368 | 265.63 | 1,293,671 | 131,954 | 184,736 | 316,691 | 21,992 | 43,985 | 65,977 | 382,668 | 29.58 |
| Lucheng District 鹿城区 | | 875,006 | 1,293,266 | 418,260 | 47.80 | 1,711,526 | 174,576 | 244,406 | 418,982 | 29,096 | 58,192 | 87,288 | 506,269 | 29.58 |
| Ouhai District 瓯海区 | | 835,607 | 996,870 | 161,263 | 19.30 | 1,158,133 | 118,130 | 165,381 | 283,511 | 19,688 | 39,377 | 59,065 | 342,576 | 29.58 |
| Pingyang County 平阳县 | | 740,448 | 761,664 | 21,216 | 2.87 | 782,880 | 58,794 | 82,312 | 141,106 | 20,746 | 41,493 | 62,239 | 203,345 | 25.97 |
| Rui'an City 瑞安市 | | 1,207,788 | 1,424,667 | 216,879 | 17.96 | 1,641,546 | 139,531 | 195,344 | 334,875 | 27,906 | 55,813 | 83,719 | 418,594 | 25.50 |
| Taishun County 泰顺县 | | 279,799 | 233,443 | -46,356 | -16.57 | 187,087 | 19,083 | 26,716 | 45,799 | 3,180 | 6,361 | 9,541 | 55,340 | 29.58 |
| Wencheng County 文成县 | | 264,878 | 212,077 | -52,801 | -19.93 | 159,276 | 16,246 | 22,745 | 38,991 | 2,708 | 5,415 | 8,123 | 47,114 | 29.58 |
| Yongjia County 永嘉县 | | 722,390 | 789,154 | 66,764 | 9.24 | 855,918 | 179,743 | 251,640 | 431,383 | 14,551 | 29,101 | 43,652 | 475,034 | 55.50 |
| Yueqing City 乐清市 | | 1,162,765 | 1,389,332 | 226,567 | 19.49 | 1,615,899 | 164,822 | 230,750 | 395,572 | 27,470 | 54,941 | 82,411 | 477,983 | 29.58 |
| | | 7,557,640 | 9,122,102 | 1,564,462 | 20.70 | 10,686,564 | 1,133,503 | 1,586,904 | 2,720,407 | 189,109 | 394,200 | 583,309 | 3,303,716 | 30.91 |
| **Zhoushan Prefecture** 舟山市 | | | | | | | | | | | | | | |
| Daishan County 岱山县 | | 197,483 | 202,164 | 4,681 | 2.37 | 206,845 | 7,095 | 9,933 | 17,027 | 3,516 | 7,033 | 10,549 | 27,577 | 13.33 |
| Dinghai District 定海区 | | 369,448 | 464,184 | 94,736 | 25.64 | 558,920 | 19,171 | 26,839 | 46,010 | 9,502 | 19,003 | 28,505 | 74,515 | 13.33 |
| Putuo District 普陀区 | | 346,237 | 378,805 | 32,568 | 9.41 | 411,373 | 14,110 | 19,754 | 33,864 | 6,993 | 13,987 | 20,980 | 54,844 | 13.33 |
| Shengsi County 嵊泗县 | | 88,362 | 76,108 | -12,254 | -13.87 | 63,854 | 2,190 | 3,066 | 5,256 | 1,086 | 2,171 | 3,257 | 8,513 | 13.33 |
| | | 1,001,530 | 1,121,261 | 119,731 | 11.95 | 1,240,992 | 42,566 | 59,592 | 102,158 | 21,097 | 42,194 | 63,291 | 165,449 | 13.33 |
| **Totals** | | 45,930,651 | 54,426,891 | 8,496,240 | 18.50 | 62,923,131 | 4,212,304 | 6,279,155 | 10,491,459 | 944,837 | 1,905,656 | 2,850,492 | 13,341,951 | 21.20 |

# *Notes*

## The China Chronicles overview

1 R. Wardlaw Thompson, *Griffith John: The Story of Fifty Years in China* (London: The Religious Tract Society, 1908), p. 65.

## Introduction

1 Leslie T. Lyall, *God Reigns in China* (London: Hodder & Stoughton, 1985), pp. 110-11.

2 Leo J. Moser, *The Chinese Mosaic: The Peoples and Provinces of China* (Boulder, CO: Westview Press, 1985), p. 33.

3 *China's Millions* (April 1878), p. 53.

4 Moser, *The Chinese Mosaic*, p. 37.

5 Marco Polo, *The Travels of Marco Polo: The Complete Yule-Cordier Edition*, Vol. 2 (New York: Dover, 1903), p. 185.

6 Polo, *The Travels of Marco Polo*, Vol. 2, pp. 185-7.

7 Moser, *The Chinese Mosaic*, p. 200.

8 Michael Buckley et al., *China: Travel Survival Kit*, 4th edition (Hawthorn, Australia: Lonely Planet, 1994), p. 423.

9 David Wang with Georgina Sam, *Christian China and the Light of the World: Miraculous Stories from China's Great Awakening* (Ventura, CA: Regal, 2013), p. 110.

## Early Christians in Zhejiang

1 L'Abbé Huc, *Christianity in China, Tartary, and Thibet*, Vol. 1 (London: Brown, Green, Longmans & Roberts, 1857), pp. 95-6.

2 Marco Polo, *The Travels of Marco Polo: The Complete Yule-Cordier Edition*, Vol. 2 (New York: Dover, 1903), p. 192.

3 A. C. Moule, *Christians in China before the Year 1550* (London: Society for Promoting Christian Knowledge, 1930), p. 242.

4 Nicolas Standaert (ed.), *Handbook of Christianity in China, Volume One: 635-1800* (Leiden: Brill, 2001), p. 386.

5 *New York Observer* (September 2, 1852), p. 283.

## 1840s

1 Arthur E. Moule, *The Story of the Cheh-Kiang Mission of the Church Missionary Society* (London: China Missionary House, 1891), p. 10.

2 G. Thompson Brown, *Earthen Vessels and Transcendent Power: American Presbyterians in China, 1837–1952* (Maryknoll, NY: Orbis, 1997), p. 31.

3 Brown, *Earthen Vessels and Transcendent Power*, p. 31.

4 G. Wright Doyle (ed.), *Builders of the Chinese Church: Pioneer Protestant Missionaries and Chinese Church Leaders* (Eugene, OR: Pickwick, 2015), p. 125.

5 Moule, *The Story of the Cheh-Kiang Mission*, p. 18.

6 Moule, *The Story of the Cheh-Kiang Mission*, p. 22.

7 Moule, *The Story of the Cheh-Kiang Mission*, p. 22.

8 Brown, *Earthen Vessels and Transcendent Power*, pp. 31-2.

9 Brown, *Earthen Vessels and Transcendent Power*, p. 33.

10 See Walter M. Lowrie, *Memoirs of the Rev. Walter M. Lowrie, Missionary to China* (New York: Carter, 1850).

## 1850s

1 Charles P. Bush, *Five Years in China, or, The Factory Boy Made a Missionary: The Life and Observations of Rev. William Aitchison, Late Missionary to China* (Philadelphia, PA: Presbyterian Board of Publication, 1865), p. 185.

2 Bush, *Five Years in China*, pp. 183-4.

3 Bush, *Five Years in China*, p. 185.

4 Robert E. Speer, *Missionary Principles and Practice* (London: Fleming H. Revell, 1902), p. 377.

5 Speer, *Missionary Principles and Practice*, p. 377.

6 Arthur E. Moule, *The Story of the Cheh-Kiang Mission of the Church Missionary Society* (London: China Missionary House, 1891), p. 54.

7 Moule, *The Story of the Cheh-Kiang Mission*, p. 55.

8 A little-known book about Stephen Dzing was published in 1868. See H. Moule, *Narrative of the Conversion of a Chinese Physician* (London: Nisbet & Co., 1868).

9 Moule, *The Story of the Cheh-Kiang Mission*, p. 149.

10 William Robson, *Griffith John: Founder of the Hankow Mission, Central China* (New York: Fleming H. Revell, 1890), p. 24.

11 Robson, *Griffith John*, pp. 24-5.

12 J. Hudson Taylor, *Looking Back: An Autobiography* (Sevenoaks, UK: OMF, 2001), p. 107.

13  Ruth A. Tucker, *From Jerusalem to Irian Jaya: A Biographical History of Christian Missions* (Grand Rapids, MI: Zondervan, 1983), p. 178.

14  Valerie Griffiths, *Not Less Than Everything: The Courageous Women Who Carried the Christian Gospel to China* (Oxford: Monarch, 2004), p. 29.

15  Tucker, *From Jerusalem to Irian Jaya*, p. 179.

16  J. C. Pollock, *Hudson Taylor and Maria: Pioneers in China* (New York: Overseas Missionary Fellowship, 1952), pp. 84–5.

17  Tucker, *From Jerusalem to Irian Jaya*, p. 180.

18  Pollock, *Hudson Taylor and Maria*, pp. 89–91.

19  Pollock, *Hudson Taylor and Maria*, pp. 89–91.

20  Pollock, *Hudson Taylor and Maria*, p. 95.

21  Cited in G. Wright Doyle (ed.), *Builders of the Chinese Church: Pioneer Protestant Missionaries and Chinese Church Leaders* (Eugene, OR: Pickwick, 2015), p. 118.

22  Dr. and Mrs. Howard J. Taylor, *J. Hudson Taylor: God's Man in China* (Chicago: Moody Press, 1978), p. 272.

23  Later volumes in the China Chronicles series will feature additional accounts of Hudson Taylor's life and ministry, with the main biography to appear in the book on Hunan Province, where he is buried.

24  Ralph D. Winter and Steven C. Hawthorne (eds), *Perspectives on the World Christian Movement* (Pasadena, CA: William Carey, 1981), p. 172.

## 1860s and 1870s

1  Duncan McLaren, *Missions of the United Presbyterian Church: The Story of Our Manchurian Mission* (Edinburgh: Offices of the United Presbyterian Church, 1896), p. 12.

2  John Butler, "Protestant Missions in the Cheh-Kiang Province," *Chinese Recorder and Missionary Journal* (July 1880), p. 289.

3  "Hang-chau Conference," *China's Millions* (August 1876), p. 176.

4  "The Native Pastor, Mr. Chu," *China's Millions* (March 1876), p. 114.

5  "Conversion of a Native Pastor," *China's Millions* (July 1875), p. 3.

6  Grace Stott, *Twenty-Six Years of Missionary Work in China* (London: Hodder & Stoughton, 1904), pp. 2–3.

7  Stott, *Twenty-Six Years of Missionary Work in China*, p. 11.

8  Danyun, *Lilies Amongst Thorns: Chinese Christians Tell Their Story through Blood and Tears* (Tonbridge, UK: Sovereign World, 1981), pp. 288–9.

9  Mrs. Meadows, "Gathering In Sheaves," *China's Millions* (August 1875), p. 23.

10  Mrs. Meadows, "Casting Away Idols," *China's Millions* (August 1875), p. 24.
11  "The Power of the Gospel," *China's Millions* (August 1875), p. 24.
12  *China's Millions* (April 1878), p. 54.
13  Mr. Meadows, "The Work in Shaohing," *China's Millions* (October 1877), p. 125.
14  W. P. Bentley, *Illustrious Chinese Christians: Biographical Sketches* (Cincinnati, OH: The Standard Publishing Company, 1906), pp. 92–3.
15  Bentley, *Illustrious Chinese Christians*, pp. 94–5.
16  Bentley, *Illustrious Chinese Christians*, p. 102.
17  "Tai-chau, Cheh-kiang Province, South-east," *China's Millions* (October 1879), p. 129.
18  W. D. Rudland, "The Story of the First Convert in Tai-chau," *China's Millions* (October 1883), p. 143.
19  Mr. Meadows, "The Work at Ning-po," *China's Millions* (April 1879), p. 48.

## 1880s

1  John Butler, "Protestant Missions in the Cheh-Kiang Province," *Chinese Recorder and Missionary Journal* (July 1880), p. 288.
2  "Message from a Chinese Pastor," *China's Millions* (December 1882), p. 151.
3  *Chinese Recorder and Missionary Journal* (June 1888), p. 289.
4  Mr. Meadows, "The Need of Prayer for Native Christians," *China's Millions* (December 1886), p. 165.
5  Mrs. George Stott, "Story of a Bible-Woman," *China's Millions* (March 1881), p. 26.
6  Mrs. George Stott, "The Troubles at Wun-chow," *China's Millions* (February 1885), p. 24.
7  Edward Hunt, "Encouragements, Difficulties, Needs, at Wen-chow," *China's Millions* (June 1907), p. 96.
8  "Death Swallowed Up in Victory," *China's Millions* (March 1881), pp. 35–6.
9  Mr. Meadows, "Examination of Chinese Converts," *China's Millions* (May 1886), p. 57.
10  Meadows, "Examination of Chinese Converts," p. 57.
11  "Report for the Year Ending May 26th, 1883," *China's Millions* (July 1883), pp. 105–11.
12  *China's Millions* (July 1889), p. 96.

## 1890s

1 Mr. Grierson, "God's Work at Wun-chau," *China's Millions* (May 1890), p. 63.

2 D. MacGillivray (ed.), *A Century of Protestant Missions in China (1807-1907)* (Shanghai: American Presbyterian Mission Press, 1907), p. 26.

3 Grace Stott, *Twenty-Six Years of Missionary Work in China* (London: Hodder & Stoughton, 1904), pp. 289-90.

4 *China's Millions* (August 1890), p. 102.

5 *China's Millions* (August-September 1891), p. 120.

6 *China's Millions* (July 1892), p. 98.

7 *China's Millions* (October 1893), p. 135.

8 *China's Millions* (September 1894), p. 115.

9 *China's Millions* (September 1895), pp. 123-4.

10 *China's Millions* (August 1897), p. 112. The sudden increase of believers in Zhejiang this year was due almost entirely to the churches in Taizhou, which baptized 630 new believers and reported a total of 1,535 members.

11 *China's Millions* (November 1899), p. 168.

12 Stott, *Twenty-Six Years of Missionary Work in China*, p. 291.

13 Stott, *Twenty-Six Years of Missionary Work in China*, p. 294.

14 "Persecution of Native Christians," *China's Millions* (October 1895), p. 148.

15 W. E. Soothill, *A Typical Mission in China* (New York: Fleming H. Revell, 1906), pp. 21-2.

16 Soothill, *A Typical Mission in China*, p. 16.

17 A. W. Douthwaite, "Fruit after Many Days—the Story of Yu Yuh-shan," *China's Millions* (January 1891), p. 4.

18 Stott, *Twenty-Six Years of Missionary Work in China*, p. 154.

19 "Presentation Banner Given to Mrs. Stott on Her Fiftieth Birthday," *China's Millions* (July 1896), p. 86.

20 Stott, *Twenty-Six Years of Missionary Work in China*, pp. 365-6.

21 See the "Table of Christians in Zhejiang" in the Appendix of this book.

## 1900s

1 Walter B. Sloan, "The Marks of Jesus," *China's Millions* (October 1900), p. 155.

2 Luella Miner, *China's Book of Martyrs: A Record of Heroic Martyrdoms and Marvelous Deliverances of Chinese Christians during the Summer of 1900* (Philadelphia, PA: Westminster Press, 1903), p. 420.

3  Miner, *China's Book of Martyrs*, p. 421.

4  "The Day before the Massacre at Kiu-chau Fu," *China's Millions* (November 1900), p. 150.

5  Ralph Coventry Forsyth (ed.), *The China Martyrs of 1900: A Complete Roll of the Christian Heroes Martyred in China in 1900, with Narratives of Survivors* (London: The Religious Tract Society, 1904), p. 92.

6  Marshall Broomhall (ed.), *Martyred Missionaries of the China Inland Mission: With a Record of the Perils and Sufferings of Some Who Escaped* (London: Morgan & Scott, 1901), p. 189.

7  Forsyth, *The China Martyrs of 1900*, p. 471.

8  Forsyth, *The China Martyrs of 1900*, p. 471.

9  Forsyth, *The China Martyrs of 1900*, pp. 92-3.

10  Forsyth, *The China Martyrs of 1900*, p. 94.

11  Forsyth, *The China Martyrs of 1900*, p. 95.

12  Broomhall, *Martyred Missionaries of the China Inland Mission*, p. 196.

13  Broomhall, *Martyred Missionaries of the China Inland Mission*, p. 197.

14  Broomhall, *Martyred Missionaries of the China Inland Mission*, p. 196.

15  Forsyth, *The China Martyrs of 1900*, p. 94.

16  Mrs. E. Hunt, "Conversions among the Women at Wun-chau," *China's Millions* (September 1901), p. 135.

17  "In Memoriam—Pastor Wang Lae-djun," *China's Millions* (May 1901), p. 75.

18  Edward Hunt, "Encouragements, Difficulties, Needs, at Wen-chow," *China's Millions* (June 1907), p. 95.

19  "News of Revival in Various Parts of China," *China's Millions* (May 1909), p. 69.

20  "Rough Summary of Statistics," *China's Millions* (July–August 1903), p. 111.

21  J. J. Meadows, "Reminiscences of the Early Days of the CIM," *China's Millions* (February 1903), pp. 68-9.

22  Bertram Wolferstan, *The Catholic Church in China* (St Louis, MO: Sands & Co., 1909), p. 450.

## 1910s and 1920s

1  George Sweeting, *More Than 2000 Great Quotes and Illustrations* (Waco, TX: Word, 1985), p. 184.

2  "In Memoriam—W. D. Rudland," *China's Millions* (March 1912), p. 44.

3  "James J. Meadows: In Loving Memory of the Senior Member of the CIM," *China's Millions* (November 1914), p. 174.

4  "James J. Meadows: In Loving Memory," p. 175.

5 "J. J. Meadows—an Appreciation," *China's Millions* (December 1914), p. 191.

6 Mr. McGhee, "Think on These Things," *China's Millions* (September 1922), p. 140.

7 Harlan P. Beach, "Recent Statistics of Missions in China," *China's Millions* (November 1905), p. 139.

8 Milton T. Stauffer (ed.), *The Christian Occupation of China* (Shanghai: China Continuation Committee, 1922), p. 54.

9 Herbert Hudson Taylor and Marshall Broomhall, *A Tamarisk Garden Blessed with Rain, or, The Autobiography of Pastor Ren* (London: China Inland Mission, 1930), pp. viii–ix.

10 For an excellent modern biography of Dora Yu, see Silas H. Wu, *Dora Yu and Christian Revival in 20th-Century China* (Boston, MA: Pishon River, 2002).

11 Dora Yu (Yu Cidu) in the Biographical Dictionary of Chinese Christianity: <http://bdcconline.net/en/stories/yu-dora>.

## 1930s

1 Jonathan Chao (ed.). *The China Mission Handbook: A Portrait of China and Its Church* (Hong Kong: Chinese Church Research Center, 1989), p. 136.

2 B. R. England, "An Ex-Bandit Evangelist," *China's Millions* (July 1933), p. 129.

3 A. K. MacPherson, "The Evolution of the Church in Yungkang," *China's Millions* (July 1937), p. 125.

4 MacPherson, "The Evolution of the Church in Yungkang," pp. 125–6.

5 G. W. Bailey, "A Genuine Revival," *China's Millions* (February 1936), p. 25.

6 Bailey, "A Genuine Revival," pp. 24–5.

7 TSPM China Prayer Calendar, 2002.

8 See the "Table of Christians in Zhejiang" in the Appendix of this book.

9 Stephen L. Sheng (trans.), *The Diaries of John Sung: An Autobiography* (Singapore: self-published, 1995), p. 34.

10 Sheng, *The Diaries of John Sung*, p. 44.

11 Sheng, *The Diaries of John Sung*, pp. 68–9.

12 Sheng, *The Diaries of John Sung*, pp. 115–16.

13 Sheng, *The Diaries of John Sung*, p. 121.

14 China Inland Mission, *Through Fire: The Story of 1938* (London: China Inland Mission, 1939), pp. 22–3.

15 China Inland Mission, *Through Fire*, pp. 24–5.

16 G. I. F. Taylor, "Remarkable Answers to Prayer," *China's Millions* (October 1939), p. 159.

17 Leslie T. Lyall, *God Reigns in China* (London: Hodder & Stoughton, 1985), p. 112.

## 1940s and 1950s

1 K. T. Gray, "God Reaches Every Class," *China's Millions* (May-June 1941), p. 44.

2 Maybeth Gray, "Where God Is Working," *China's Millions* (May-June 1949), p. 32.

3 *China Study Journal* (December 1992).

4 Leslie T. Lyall, *God Reigns in China* (London: Hodder & Stoughton, 1985), pp. 112-14.

5 Leslie T. Lyall, *The Phoenix Rises: The Phenomenal Growth of Eight Chinese Churches* (Singapore: Overseas Missionary Fellowship, 1992), p. 66.

6 See the chapter "Miao Zizhong—the Cedar of Lebanon" in this book.

7 Lyall, *The Phoenix Rises*, pp. 66-8.

8 Lyall, *The Phoenix Rises*, p. 69.

9 *China Study Journal* (December 1992).

## 1960s

1 Leslie T. Lyall, *Red Sky at Night: Communism Confronts Christianity in China* (London: Hodder & Stoughton, 1969), pp. 36-7.

2 Zhang Rongliang with Eugene Bach, *I Stand with Christ: The Courageous Life of a Chinese Christian* (New Kensington, PA: Whitaker House, 2015), p. 59.

3 Leslie T. Lyall, *God Reigns in China* (London: Hodder & Stoughton, 1985), p. 168.

4 Leslie T. Lyall, *The Phoenix Rises: The Phenomenal Growth of Eight Chinese Churches* (Singapore: Overseas Missionary Fellowship, 1992), pp. 68-9.

5 Lyall, *The Phoenix Rises*, p. 72.

6 "Trial by Fire," *China and the Church Today* (November-December 1983), p. 10.

7 "Trial by Fire," p. 10.

8 "Trial by Fire," p. 11.

9 "Trial by Fire," p. 11.

10 DC Talk and The Voice of the Martyrs, *Jesus Freaks: Stories of Those Who Stood for Jesus*, Vol. 2 (Minneapolis, MN: Bethany House, 2002), n.p.

11   Carl Lawrence, *The Church in China* (Minneapolis, MN: Bethany House, 1985), p. 43.
12   See Daniel chapter 3.
13   Lawrence, *The Church in China*, p. 43.
14   See Acts 9.26-28.
15   Lyall, *The Phoenix Rises*, p. 70.
16   G. Wright Doyle (ed.), *Builders of the Chinese Church: Pioneer Protestant Missionaries and Chinese Church Leaders* (Eugene, OR: Pickwick, 2015), p. 2.

## 1970s

1   "My Experience of a Hidden Church Meeting," *Pray for China* (April 1979).
2   "A Christian Funeral in Chekiang," *Pray for China* (November 1974).
3   "The Spirit of God at Work in China," *Pray for China* (June 1976), pp. 2-4.
4   "The Spirit of God at Work in China," p. 3.
5   Jonathan Chao, *Wise as Serpents, Harmless as Doves* (Pasadena, CA: William Carey Library, 1988), pp. 28-9.
6   Chao, *Wise as Serpents, Harmless as Doves*, p. 30.
7   Chao, *Wise as Serpents, Harmless as Doves*, p. 30.
8   Danyun, *Lilies Amongst Thorns: Chinese Christians Tell Their Story through Blood and Tears* (Tonbridge, UK: Sovereign World, 1981), pp. 304-5.
9   Danyun, *Lilies Amongst Thorns*, pp. 305-6.
10   Danyun, *Lilies Amongst Thorns*, pp. 303-4.
11   Leslie T. Lyall, *God Reigns in China* (London: Hodder & Stoughton, 1985), pp. 168-9.
12   Chao, *Wise as Serpents, Harmless as Doves*, pp. 99-100.

## 1980s

1   Alan Hunter and Kim-Kwong Chan, *Protestantism in Contemporary China*, Cambridge Studies in Ideology and Religion (New York: Cambridge University Press, 1993), p. 211.
2   Hunter and Chan, *Protestantism in Contemporary China*, p. 214.
3   Accounts of the Dongyang and Yiwu persecutions were distributed throughout China and ultimately published overseas, including by *Asian Report* (July 1982).
4   Tony Lambert, *The Resurrection of the Chinese Church* (Wheaton, IL: Harold Shaw, 1994), p. 86.

5 "What Is Your Name, Doctor?" *Asian Report* (January–February 1985).
6 "What Is Your Name, Doctor?"
7 Peter Xu Yongze, personal communication, October 2003.
8 Ding Hei, personal communication, March 2001.
9 Brother Yun with Paul Hattaway, *The Heavenly Man: The Remarkable True Story of Chinese Christian Brother Yun* (London: Monarch, 2002), p. 193.
10 *Bridge* (March–April 1984).
11 *Pray for China* (January–February 1986); Lambert, *The Resurrection of the Chinese Church*, p. 143, estimated a total of 2.5 million Evangelical believers in Zhejiang at the time.
12 Tony Lambert, *China's Christian Millions: The Costly Revival* (London: Monarch, 1999), p. 142.
13 Leslie T. Lyall, *The Phoenix Rises: The Phenomenal Growth of Eight Chinese Churches* (Singapore: Overseas Missionary Fellowship, 1992), pp. 133–4.

## Miao Zizhong—the Cedar of Lebanon

1 Danyun, *Lilies Amongst Thorns: Chinese Christians Tell Their Story through Blood and Tears* (Tonbridge, UK: Sovereign World, 1981), p. 9.
2 Danyun, *Lilies Amongst Thorns*, p. 10.
3 Danyun, *Lilies Amongst Thorns*, pp. 11–12.
4 Paraphrased from Danyun, *Lilies Amongst Thorns*, p. 12.
5 Danyun, *Lilies Amongst Thorns*, p. 13.
6 Danyun, *Lilies Amongst Thorns*, p. 15.
7 Danyun, *Lilies Amongst Thorns*, p. 18.
8 Danyun, *Lilies Amongst Thorns*, p. 19.

## 1990s

1 *China News and Church Report* (November 22, 1991).
2 *China Notes* (Spring and Summer 1990).
3 Amity News Service, April 1994.
4 Cited in Tony Lambert, *China's Christian Millions: The Costly Revival* (London: Monarch, 1999), p. 202.
5 "The Vincentian Missions of China (14th Year)," 1937.
6 Chinese Academy of Social Sciences, Beijing, 1992.
7 Ji Zhongwen in *Zongjiao* [Religion], cited in OMF International, "The Local Church," *China Insight* (July–August 1998).
8 Lambert, *China's Christian Millions*, p. 163.

9   Lambert, *China's Christian Millions*, pp. 163-5.
10  Su Shan, "The Children of the Kingdom," *Asian Report* (March-April 1993), p. 3.
11  "Reaching and Teaching," *Asian Report* (July-September 1992), p. 20.
12  *China News and Church Report* (August 9, 1996). See also *Open Doors News Brief* (August 1996).
13  Compass Direct, July 1997.
14  "Only by Grace," *Asian Report* (April 1996), pp. 8-9.
15  Peter Xu Yongze, personal communication, October 2003.
16  Ding Hei, personal communication, March 2001.
17  Far East Broadcasting, May 1991.
18  Far East Broadcasting, June 1992.
19  Far East Broadcasting, June 1992.
20  Far East Broadcasting, April 1995.
21  Far East Broadcasting, August 1995.
22  Compass Direct, December 1996.
23  Compass Direct, November 1997.
24  Far East Broadcasting, October 1998.
25  Trans World Radio, September 1998.
26  Compass Direct, December 1998.

## 2000s

1   "An Overview of the Church in Zhejiang Province," *Lift Up Our Holy Hands* (February-March 2000).
2   John Pomfret, "Evangelicals on the Rise in the Land of Mao," *Washington Post* (December 24, 2002).
3   *Pray for China* (April-May 1999).
4   Far East Broadcasting, October 2001.
5   David Aikman, *Jesus in Beijing: How Christianity Is Transforming China and Changing the Global Balance of Power* (Washington DC: Regnery, 2003), pp. 180-1.
6   *Wenzhou Daily* (December 12, 2000).
7   *Global Chinese Ministries* (June 2007).
8   Paul Golf with Pastor Lee, *The Coming Chinese Church: How Rising Faith in China is Spilling Over Its Boundaries* (Oxford: Monarch, 2013), pp. 167-8.
9   *Time* (August 28, 2006).
10  Patrick Johnstone and Jason Mandryk, *Operation World: 21st Century Edition* (Carlisle: Paternoster Lifestyle, 2001), p. 181.
11  Far East Broadcasting, April 2000.

12 Far East Broadcasting, May 2000.
13 *Global Chinese Ministries* (March 2001).
14 *Lift Up Our Holy Hands* (December 2001).
15 Far East Broadcasting, July 2001.
16 Far East Broadcasting, July 2001.
17 Far East Broadcasting, January 2002.
18 Far East Broadcasting, September 2002.
19 Far East Broadcasting, September 2002.
20 Compass Direct, March 2005.
21 *Antioch Missions* (June 2006).
22 Open Doors, Autumn 2006.
23 *Lift Up Our Holy Hands* (November 2007).
24 *Lift Up Our Holy Hands* (April 2008).
25 *Pray for China* (April-May 2009).

## 2010s

1 Brent Fulton, *China's Urban Christians: A Light that Cannot be Hidden* (Eugene, OR: Pickwick, 2015), p. 51.
2 David Wang with Georgina Sam, *Christian China and the Light of the World: Miraculous Stories from China's Great Awakening* (Ventura, CA: Regal, 2013), p. 162.
3 "Prayer Center Destroyed by Force," *China Aid* (September 1, 2010).
4 The report and video can be viewed at: <www.cnn.com/2014/09/15/world/asia/china-christians-church>.
5 "Why Crosses? Why Zhejiang?" *ChinaSource* (August 24, 2016).
6 "Wenzhou Christians Hold Service in Church Ruins after Brutal Demolition," *China Aid* (June 13, 2016).
7 David Aikman, *Jesus in Beijing: How Christianity Is Transforming China and Changing the Global Balance of Power* (Washington DC: Regnery, 2003), p. 185.
8 Aikman, *Jesus in Beijing*, p. 186.
9 Dennis Balcombe, personal communication, September 2006.
10 Dennis Balcombe, personal communication, September 2006.
11 "Wenzhou Pastor Ousted from Position, Loses Preaching Certificate," *China Aid* (November 18, 2016).
12 Stoyan Zaimov, "Chinese Pastor Re-Arrested in Highest Profile Case Targeting Christians since Cultural Revolution," *The Christian Post* (January 12, 2017).
13 Far East Broadcasting, May 2013.
14 Letter to Asia Harvest from Lanxi, Zhejiang Province, September 2012.

15  See Christian Shepherd and Stella Qiu, "In China's Jerusalem, Christians Say Faith Trumps Official Sunday School Ban," *Reuters World News* (December 24, 2017).

16  See "Conditions Unknown after 14 Vanished Christians Released," *China Aid* (February 16, 2018).

17  Samuel Smith, "China Trying to 'Rewrite the Bible,' Force Christians to Sing Communist Anthems," *The Christian Post* (September 28, 2018).

18  "China: Christian Schoolchildren Forced to Tick 'No Religion' Box," *The Christian Post* (October 6, 2018).

# Selected bibliography

Aikman, David, *Jesus in Beijing: How Christianity Is Transforming China and Changing the Global Balance of Power* (Washington DC: Regnery, 2003).

Bentley, W. P., *Illustrious Chinese Christians: Biographical Sketches* (Cincinnati, OH: The Standard Publishing Company, 1906).

Broomhall, A. J., *Hudson Taylor and China's Open Century, Book Five: Refiner's Fire* (London: Overseas Missionary Fellowship, 1985).

Broomhall, Marshall (ed.), *Martyred Missionaries of the China Inland Mission: With a Record of the Perils and Sufferings of Some Who Escaped* (London: Morgan & Scott, 1901).

Brown, G. Thompson, *Earthen Vessels and Transcendent Power: American Presbyterians in China, 1837–1952* (Maryknoll, NY: Orbis, 1997).

Bush, Charles P., *Five Years in China, or, The Factory Boy Made a Missionary: The Life and Observations of Rev. William Aitchison, Late Missionary to China* (Philadelphia, PA: Presbyterian Board of Publication, 1865).

Cao, Nanlai, *Constructing China's Jerusalem: Christians, Power, and Place in Contemporary Wenzhou*, Contemporary Issues in Asia and the Pacific (Stanford, CA: Stanford University Press, 2010).

Chao, Jonathan, *Wise as Serpents, Harmless as Doves* (Pasadena, CA: William Carey Library, 1988).

China Inland Mission, *Through Fire: The Story of 1938* (London: China Inland Mission, 1939).

Danyun, *Lilies Amongst Thorns: Chinese Christians Tell Their Story through Blood and Tears* (Tonbridge, UK: Sovereign World, 1981).

Doyle, G. Wright (ed.), *Builders of the Chinese Church: Pioneer Protestant Missionaries and Chinese Church Leaders* (Eugene, OR: Pickwick, 2015).

Forsyth, Ralph Coventry (ed.), *The China Martyrs of 1900: A Complete Roll of the Christian Heroes Martyred in China in 1900, with Narratives of Survivors* (London: The Religious Tract Society, 1904).

Golf, Paul, with Pastor Lee, *The Coming Chinese Church: How Rising Faith in China is Spilling Over Its Boundaries* (Oxford: Monarch, 2013).

Griffiths, Valerie, *Not Less Than Everything: The Courageous Women Who Carried the Christian Gospel to China* (Oxford: Monarch, 2004).

Gruché, Kingston de, *Doctor Apricot of "Heaven-Below": The Story of the Hangchow Medical Mission* (London: Fleming H. Revell, 1911).

# Selected bibliography

Hunter, Alan, and Kim-Kwong Chan, *Protestantism in Contemporary China*, Cambridge Studies in Ideology and Religion (New York: Cambridge University Press, 1993).

Lambert, Tony, *China's Christian Millions: The Costly Revival* (London: Monarch, 1999).

——, *The Resurrection of the Chinese Church* (Wheaton, IL: Harold Shaw, 1994).

Lawrence, Carl, *The Church in China* (Minneapolis, MN: Bethany House, 1985).

Lowrie, Walter M., *Memoirs of the Rev. Walter M. Lowrie, Missionary to China* (New York: Carter, 1850).

Lyall, Leslie T., *God Reigns in China* (London: Hodder & Stoughton, 1985).

——, *The Phoenix Rises: The Phenomenal Growth of Eight Chinese Churches* (Singapore: Overseas Missionary Fellowship, 1992).

——, *Red Sky at Night: Communism Confronts Christianity in China* (London: Hodder & Stoughton, 1969).

MacGillivray, D. (ed.), *A Century of Protestant Missions in China (1807-1907)* (Shanghai: American Presbyterian Mission Press, 1907).

Miner, Luella, *China's Book of Martyrs: A Record of Heroic Martyrdoms and Marvelous Deliverances of Chinese Christians during the Summer of 1900* (Philadelphia, PA: Westminster Press, 1903).

Moule, A. C., *Christians in China before the Year 1550* (London: Society for Promoting Christian Knowledge, 1930).

Moule, Arthur E., *Half a Century in China: Recollections and Observations* (London: Hodder & Stoughton, 1911).

——, *New China and Old: Personal Recollections and Observations of Thirty Years* (London: Seeley, Service & Co., 1902).

——, *The Story of the Cheh-Kiang Mission of the Church Missionary Society* (London: China Missionary House, 1891).

Moule, H., *Narrative of the Conversion of a Chinese Physician* (London: Nisbet & Co., 1868).

Nevius, Helen C. S., *The Life of John Livingston Nevius, for Forty Years a Missionary in China* (New York: Fleming H. Revell, 1895).

——, *Our Life in China* (New York: Robert Carter & Bros., 1891).

Nevius, John L., *Methods of Mission Work* (Shanghai: American Presbyterian Mission Press, 1895).

Pollock, J. C., *Hudson Taylor and Maria: Pioneers in China* (New York: Overseas Missionary Fellowship, 1952).

Robson, William, *Griffith John: Founder of the Hankow Mission, Central China* (New York: Fleming H. Revell, 1890).

# Selected bibliography

Sheng, Stephen L. (trans.), *The Diaries of John Sung: An Autobiography* (Singapore: self-published, 1995).

Soothill, W. E., *A Typical Mission in China* (New York: Fleming H. Revell, 1906).

Speer, Robert E., *A Missionary Pioneer in the Far East: A Memorial of Divie Bethune McCartee* (New York: Fleming H. Revell, 1922).

Stauffer, Milton T. (ed.), *The Christian Occupation of China* (Shanghai: China Continuation Committee, 1922).

Stott, Grace, *Twenty-Six Years of Missionary Work in China* (London: Hodder & Stoughton, 1904).

Taylor, Herbert Hudson, and Marshall Broomhall, *A Tamarisk Garden Blessed with Rain, or, The Autobiography of Pastor Ren* (London: China Inland Mission, 1930).

Taylor, Dr. and Mrs. Howard J., *J. Hudson Taylor: God's Man in China* (Chicago: Moody Press, 1978).

Taylor, J. Hudson, *Looking Back: An Autobiography* (Sevenoaks, UK: OMF, 2001).

Thompson, R. Wardlaw, *Griffith John: The Story of Fifty Years in China* (London: The Religious Tract Society, 1908).

Wang, David, with Georgina Sam, *Christian China and the Light of the World: Miraculous Stories from China's Great Awakening* (Ventura, CA: Regal, 2013).

Wu, Silas H., *Dora Yu and Christian Revival in 20th-Century China* (Boston, MA: Pishon River, 2002).

Yun, Brother, with Paul Hattaway, *The Heavenly Man: The Remarkable True Story of Chinese Christian Brother Yun* (London: Monarch, 2002).

# Contact details

———••———

Paul Hattaway is the founder and director of Asia Harvest, a non-denominational ministry that serves the Church in Asia through various strategic initiatives, including Bible printing and supporting Asian missionaries who share the gospel among unreached peoples.

The author can be reached by email at <**paul@asiaharvest. org**>, or by writing to him via any of the addresses listed below.

For more than 30 years Asia Harvest has served the Church in Asia through strategic projects that equip the local churches. At the time of going to print, Asia Harvest has successfully distributed more than 700,000 Bibles to house church Christians in Zhejiang Province, in addition to supporting many evangelists and providing aid to hundreds of persecuted church leaders and their families.

If you would like to receive the free Asia Harvest newsletter or to order other volumes in the China Chronicles series or Paul's other books, please visit <**www.asiaharvest.org**> or write to the address below nearest you:

**Asia Harvest USA and Canada**
353 Jonestown Rd #320
Winston-Salem, NC 27104
USA

**Asia Harvest Australia**
36 Nelson Street
Stepney, SA 5069
Australia

**Asia Harvest New Zealand**
PO Box 1757
Queenstown, 9348
New Zealand

**Asia Harvest UK and Ireland**
c/o AsiaLink
PO Box 891
Preston PR4 9AB
United Kingdom

**Asia Harvest Europe**
c/o Stiftung SALZ
Moehringer Landstr. 98
70563 Stuttgart
Germany